FALLING
FOR A LIE

New Age beliefs nearly killed me

JAY CHRISTIAN
as told to Helen Heavirland

Pacific Press® Publishing Association
Nampa, Idaho
Oshawa, Ontario, Canada

Edited by Kenneth R. Wade
Designed by Michelle C. Petz

Copyright © 1998 by
Pacific Press® Publishing Association
Printed in the United States
All Rights Reserved

Holm, Jon C.
    Falling for a lie : New Age beliefs nearly killed me /
Jay Christian, as told to Helen Heavirland.
        p.   cm.
    Includes bibliographical references.
    ISBN 0-8163-1646-5 (alk. paper)
    1. New Age movement—Controversial literature.   2.
Christian, Jay.
I. Heavirland, Helen, 1946-   . II. Title.
BP605.N48C55   1998
239'.93—dc21   97-47666
                                                        CIP

98 99 00 01 02 • 5 4 3 2 1

Dedication

Jay:
To my wife, Annette,
whose gentle and loving spirit is a shining light in my life.
To my daughters, Jodi and Cari,
of whom I am very proud.
And to Inki,
who was truly my best friend.

Helen:
To my friend and mentor, the late VeraLee Wiggins,
who believed in me.

Special thanks to writers who helped hone various chapters and to Pastor Owen Bandy, Pastor and Mrs. John Riggs, Marcia Thompson, and Sandy Zaugg who read the manuscript and made valuable suggestions. The authors bear the responsibility for any weaknesses that still sneaked by.

Special thanks to Sandy Zaugg who made her attic room Helen's during critical writing periods.

Special thanks to Ken Wade who edited with vision, tact, and patience.

Special thanks to all who blanketed us with prayer.

Jay Christian
Helen Heavirland

The places, radio stations, and events of this story are true. Most names have been changed to protect anonymity of individuals. Actual names are used for Jay, Jodi, Annette, Cari, Pastor Riggs, and public figures.

Table of Contents

Chapter One

Promise

"Where are you, God?" I threw the words at blue sky. A storm raged within. "Do you know Jay Christian exists? Do you care?"

Gulls screamed.

I ran again, my long legs beating the sand. Questions, as vicious as El Niño waves, crashed into my mind. *What does "the fall" mean? When will it happen? Why? Why has it harassed me so long? Will I ever find answers? Will my life ever make sense?*

Crushed in spirit, I collapsed on the beach. A breeze cooled me. Gulls zigzagged the sky. They skittered about the beach or rose and fell on waves. They floated freely on the breeze.

Wouldn't I love to take off! I thought. *To fly!*

I shook my head. *Fly? Why did I even think it?*

Flying raised the other issue that haunted me. Or was it a separate issue? Were they related?

I ran back toward my car, unable to outpace the questions. They stalked me. Here. Everywhere.

Falling for a Lie

As soon as I got home, I washed and polished my green '68 Camaro Super Sport 350. As much as I loved the beach, I wasn't about to take any chance of the salt air damaging one of the very few things that brought me any joy. While I shined the mag rims, an older couple from an apartment near mine walked down the sidewalk. Our eyes met as they neared. She smiled. He dipped his head and greeted me.

"Good afternoon," I responded.

They stopped. We chatted a bit. Small talk. Something came up about the evening.

"We're going to a class," she enthused. "Self-hypnosis. It's helping me tremendously!"

"You should o' seen the difference," her husband added. "She was totally crippled. In a wheelchair." He smiled and motioned proudly toward his wife. "Look at her now! Out walking!"

"So, what made the difference?" I asked.

"I use self-hypnosis to will my mind to heal my body," she explained. "You can see it's working."

"Do they teach anything about former lives?" I questioned.

"Yeah, they talk a lot about reincarnation. Why do you ask?"

"Oh . . ." I sighed. My thoughts drifted off. Just remembering, terror built inside me again. The experience had haunted my childhood. It was more vivid than a dream. I sensed it as a real experience. *Was it sometime in my past? Will it happen in the future? Is there some way to figure out what's going to happen to me before it actually occurs?*

I'd searched for answers. At twelve, the troubling questions and my insatiable curiosity made me eager to join my church's class to study the Bible and church history. Two verses into Genesis, the pastor acknowledged my raised hand. "What does 'without form and void' mean?" Before the chapter was out, I asked, "So if God created us in His image, how can we have a body and Him not have one?" Shortly, "Who did Cain marry? Where did she come from?"

Before long I noticed that whenever I waved my hand, the pastor rolled his eyes, then took a deep breath. "Yes?" he asked. But each time, the message in his sigh grew clearer—"Oh no! Not him again!"

I felt put down. But I wanted answers. Didn't God have them?

I persisted. But often the pastor's answers didn't make sense to me. And when I asked another question to try to understand, he sighed deep and long and in a firm, exasperated voice, answered, "You just have to believe." That was OK once in a while. But over and over again?

Finally, we reached the Gospels. I believed Jesus was the Son of God and I had a picture in my mind of what He was like. Had I misunderstood? The Jesus I heard about here was a weak, weird doormat. I wasn't impressed.

I'd learned from childhood that God could help people make sense out of life. Why wouldn't He help me?

The man cleared his throat.

Startled, I brought my thoughts back to the sunny afternoon in Long Beach, California. "Well," I said, "a lot of years ago I had an experience I've always wondered about."

"Why don't you come with us to the class?" the husband invited.

"Can't hurt," his wife added. "Tonight's the beginning of a new class."

"I'm off work tonight," I said. "Why not?"

While I finished polishing the rims, memories pushed in on me again.

As a teenager, I had prayed for answers to the haunting experience. But answers didn't come and the questions left over from the

Falling for a Lie

Bible class needled my sense of reason. *How could God direct the slaughter of innocent people just because they worshiped other gods? Why didn't God just wipe everyone off the earth and start over after Adam and Eve sinned? How could God condemn people to burn in eternal hell just because they didn't do exactly as He wanted?*

By the time I hit six-foot-five-inches, my questions had grown too. What kind of a God is He, anyway? Selfish? Self-centered? On some kind of ego trip?

On Sundays I sometimes went to church with various girlfriends. But the differences bugged me—all these religions claimed to follow the same Bible, but different churches surely got different things out of it. Then I noticed that sometimes a preacher would talk about a Bible text as if it said one thing, but when I read the verses before and after it, it really said something else. Sometimes just the opposite. I asked several different pastors about the discrepancies after the service. They fumbled, then came up with justification from doctrines. But their answers didn't make sense to me when I compared them with what the Bible said.

Questioning preachers became my Sunday morning entertainment. "How can Jesus make and drink wine and yet talk against it?" "If God is love, how can He condemn people to eternal hell?" "If life goes on after we die, were we alive before we were born?"

Later I'd laugh. But it was a hollow, sad laugh. *God, if the answers aren't in church, where do I look?* I prayed.

By the time I went into the army, I was mad at God. Through Fort Ord, Camp Roberts, and Korea, I left God alone and guessed He did the same for me. Whenever the frustrating memories surfaced, I buried them as quickly as possible.

After disc jockey school in Atlanta Georgia, I'd scoured Southern California for a job in radio. KJLH-FM, an adult easy listening station, had an opening. I cringed when I discovered its broadcast studio was in a Long Beach mortuary. "We're Number One among the dead," the manager joked during my interview.

And tonight, the first night of a new self-hypnosis class, is my night off. Even though I haven't paid any attention to God for several years, maybe He hasn't forgotten me. Maybe He remembers my questions. Maybe this class will provide answers . . . solid answers that can lead me into the future with confidence instead of fear.

That evening I rode with the older couple to a home in a nice neighborhood in North Hollywood. Thirty people gathered in the study. The teacher—a man about sixty—sat behind a big, imposing desk. The lights were off, but candles glowed from everywhere— bookcases, windowsills, end tables. The hair on the back of my neck stood on end. It felt eerie, but exciting.

"The purpose of these classes," the teacher started out, "is to help you learn self-hypnosis. Through this wonder, you'll be able to get in touch with your soul, to gain control of your life, and, if you are so inclined, to experience former lives."

I was so inclined. But I also felt skeptical . . . and nervous. "When I experience a former life," I told my new friends on the way home, "I'll believe it."

Chapter Two

Now What?

"You can't do self-hypnosis until you learn to totally relax," the teacher said. Looking forward to experiencing regression, I practiced the techniques daily.

During the next sessions the teacher talked more about love than about any other single thing—"the true love of God, Jesus, Buddha, and other people of God." He stressed love of God, love for God, love for fellow humans, love for nature, love for animals, love for everything. Finally, here was a group of people who expressed love much the same way as I pictured the Bible advocating. I drank it in.

"What about the Bible?" a young woman asked one evening in class. "Is it worth anything?"

She'd voiced a question I'd wondered about. I listened closely.

"The Bible is a good book," the teacher answered. "It has helped many people. But the Bible is thousands of years old." He paused and smiled at the young woman. "Would you want to get rid of your car and go back to riding a donkey?"

"No," she responded. "I think I'll keep my Mustang."

Everyone laughed.

She looked puzzled for an instant, then realized what she'd said. "The Ford kind," she added, giggling.

The teacher continued, "Knowledge has multiplied since the Bible was written. Society has moved forward. We know much more in science, in mathematics, in technology. We also know much more about the spirit."

"So is the Bible wrong?" an older man on the other side of the room asked.

"No, no. Not wrong," the teacher said. "It's fine, as far as it goes. It's just that we've moved on and now we know so much more."

Just like a reading book, I thought. *A first-grade reader has words like "the" and "run" and "what" and "look." Every week there are new words to learn. Knowledge increases. But whether you're in seventh grade or graduate school, the basic first-grade words are still valid. They're always spelled the same. And they mean the same thing.*

I was relieved by the teacher's response. Even though I hadn't been able to find the answers I needed in the Bible, I'd always felt it was important. Now I could continue to respect it but still grow beyond it. *Is this class God's answer to my infrequent prayers?* I wondered.

Besides enjoying the love I felt while at the class, I concentrated on the relaxation and self-hypnosis techniques the instructor taught. At home, I practiced faithfully.

"You're having trouble getting very deep, aren't you?" the teacher asked me one evening.

"Yes," I admitted.

"You have an analytical mind, don't you?"

"Yes."

Falling for a Lie

"It will be harder for you than for some, but you'll get to the place where you can go deeply enough into meditation that you can regress into past lives. Just keep practicing. Concentrate on the relaxation techniques."

A few sessions later, the teacher looked directly at me. "Are you ready?"

"Eager," I answered. I sat in a chair in front of his desk.

"Always pray first," the teacher advised, "for protection." He bowed his head. "God, guide our excursion. Keep us safe from evil spirit influences. Amen."

Then he turned to me. "You've already been practicing self-hypnosis?"

"Yes."

"To experience regression, you'll need to go to deeper levels."

"OK."

"Like we've talked about before, some people see numbers in their head as they progress deeper into hypnosis. Others see rulers or yardsticks, thermometers, or there are other ways to determine the level of hypnosis. What's it been for you?"

"Just numbers."

"Fine."

He directed me to place my palms flat on the desk and my forehead on the desktop between my hands. As soon as I did, numbers flashed by me—20, 30, 32, 34, 36. I'd never before been so deep into hypnosis. A tingle went up my spine.

"You've got to go deeper," he said.

I tried, but was stalled at 36. The teacher touched the tips of his middle fingers to mine. A jolt of electricity burst into my fingers and shot through my body. *Whoosh*. I plunged deeper and deeper. Numbers raced by—40 . . . 46 . . . 52 . . . 60.

"We'll start out with the present and work our way back," the

Now What?

teacher explained. He suggested an age and I settled on a memory about it. Then we went back a couple years and repeated the process.

Shortly, though totally aware of my present surroundings, in my mind I saw the house where I first lived. I looked over it, saw the house plan, and remembered some family scenes. We'd moved from that house about the time I turned four. I never saw it again. The few memories I'd had of it were vague, at best. Yet, here I was, twenty years later, taking a detailed tour.

"Go back further," the instructor said. "Keep going back . . . and back."

Page 15

The scenes of the house faded. Total blackness took their place for a few seconds. Suddenly, I was falling . . . off a very tall building. Red brick walls and windows with small panes flashed by as gravity pulled me down . . . down . . . down. . . . Terror gripped me.

I exploded straight up out of my chair. The teacher jumped. Everyone in the room caught their breath or gasped. "No!" I screamed. "Not there!" My heart pounded like it might leap out of my chest.

I'd been there before. As a toddler. One night I was lying in my crib. Just starting to doze. All of a sudden I was falling off a huge, very tall building. Red brick walls and windows with small panes flashed by as I tumbled down . . . down . . . down. . . . Terror gripped me. Heart pounding, I jumped up, grabbed the crib railing, and screamed at the top of my lungs.

The fall had haunted me. Terrified me.

Now, the teacher reached up for my hand. "Relax," he soothed. "No harm will come to you."

Trembling, I folded back into the chair. My heart pounded in my head. The teacher motioned toward his assistant. Jeff, a slim, professional-looking man probably in his early thirties pulled a chair up on my right side. "Jeff and I will travel with you into your memories as protectors. If you need us, we'll be there to warn you of dangers or to help you understand what you see."

I leaned forward, my pulse still racing.

"Can we go back to that memory as long as Jeff and I go with you?" he asked.

"No! Not that one!"

"OK. That'll be fine," he said. "Just go past that memory. Past all the blackness. Keep going back until you settle on a happy, peaceful time."

After a short period of darkness, I saw myself looking down at my feet. I wore scruffy cowboy boots and dirty old chaps. To my left, old wild-west-type buildings lined the wooden sidewalk. On my right, horses and buggies swerved around mud puddles in the dirt street. A gas lantern topped an octagon-shaped wooden pole.

As the vision continued, I described part of what was happening. But I purposely left out significant parts. The teacher had said he and Jeff would go with me. Would they really see everything I saw? Was this for real?

It certainly felt real. I walked down the sidewalk to the corner, stepped onto a square wooden step down into the street, and crossed to the restaurant on the far side.

An attractive waitress, probably in her early twenties, with light brown hair pulled into a bun at the back of her head came to take my order. I flashed her a smile. She gave only a business-like response. I tried to make small talk. Nothing. "What's a pretty girl like you doing in a place like this?" Zip! I felt miffed that she didn't respond. Defeated, I ordered stew and ale.

Since nothing much happened while I waited for my meal, I had a chance to think from my present perspective. Why was I expecting her to be attracted to me?

Now What?

Immediately a picture popped into mind. I was in my late twenties to early thirties, muscular, about five feet ten inches tall, with slicked-back jet black hair, dark eyes, and a somewhat pointed nose. Frankly, I was rather handsome.

When the waitress brought my meal, I pulled out all the stops. Zilch. She was probably one of those finicky people who insisted everyone be clean and odor-free, anyway, and not ready for a cowboy used to lots of physical work. I ate my meal, paid for it, and retraced my steps to the place where I entered the vision.

From that spot, I turned right into a hotel and climbed a narrow staircase. At the top of the stairs I turned right again and entered the first door on the right. In my room, I walked over to a wooden-framed, oval mirror. The reflection perfectly matched the picture that had come to my mind earlier. Dumbfounded, I stared at my image.

Then I turned and walked over to the bed, lay on it with my boots up on the footboard, and went to sleep.

At that point, the vision faded.

"What were the lampposts like?" I asked.

"They were wood," the teacher said, "and octagonal. They were large at the bottom and top and tapered to a smaller diameter in the middle."

He was right.

"What was the restaurant shaped like?" I asked.

"The side walls ran straight along the wooden walks," he said, "but they didn't come clear to the corner. It was like the corner of the building was snubbed off and there was a diagonal wall back ten or twelve feet from where the sidewalks met. That left a covered, triangle porch. The door was in the middle of the diagonal wall."

"Uh-huh." This was eerie. "Would you describe my hotel

room?" I asked.

"From where you entered," he said, "on the left wall was an oval, wooden-framed mirror. Under it was a wooden stand with a bowl and pitcher. The bed's metal headboard was up against the outside wall. On the right was a small window and then a chair."

That night I went home with more questions than I'd considered in a long while. *The fall off the tall building. It was the exact thing I'd seen and felt as a toddler. And I'd never told anyone about the experience. What was it? Why has it affected my life so profoundly?*

And who was I in those former lives? Was this experience for real? Did God lead me to this class to help me make sense out of my life? Why didn't the Bible classes teach me about these things?

Earlier I had said that if I ever experienced a former life, I'd believe in reincarnation. Now what?

Chapter Three

Souls at Work

The morning after the regression, I pondered the experience.

Something real happened. It wasn't like I was dreaming or daydreaming. I was fully aware of the room, the people around me, the sounds, and the silence. Yet I was living in a former time and a different place. Actually experiencing it.

But how could it be real? It was totally foreign from anything I'd ever learned before. Wasn't it "spiritual"? Why didn't they ever talk about experiences like this in any church I'd ever gone to? Did the Bible talk about it?

Bits and pieces of a Bible story came to mind—something about Israel's King Saul going to a witch to talk to the dead prophet, Samuel, and Saul being condemned for it.

But surely that was different . . . wasn't it? I just want to know what to expect from the future. Huh . . . that's what Saul wanted. But if I could just know tomorrow, I could be prepared for it.

Why did I feel like I was rationalizing?

Falling for a Lie

A knock at the door interrupted my reverie. The neighbors who had invited me to the self-hypnosis class greeted me. The wife got right down to business. "We noticed you looked a little puzzled last night. Thought maybe you had questions."

"I do," I replied.

She offered a thick, well-worn paperback. "We brought you one of our books about Edgar Cayce."

As I reached for it, she continued, "Edgar Cayce is called the Sleeping Prophet. He died in 1945, but his experiences have helped us tremendously!"

Her husband broke in, "They helped us understand how God originated life on earth, how souls become trapped in flesh, and how to use spiritual powers to change things as you want them."

"And that's why I'm walking now!" his wife enthused.

I accepted the book gratefully and began reading. A negative, depressing feeling settled over me. Snippets of long-forgotten Bible verses crossed my mind—wizards, familiar spirits. Do not go to them.

But hypnosis had obviously helped my neighbor. I wanted desperately to make sense of my experiences. I wanted to learn how to see my own future and how to prepare for it.

Besides, the people at the class were so accepting. I craved their love.

I kept attending classes, kept meditating, kept reading. The more I got involved, the less the thoughts from the Bible bothered me.

Edgar Cayce's life fascinated me. The visions. His dedication to helping people reach their higher selves. I devoured the book and borrowed another.

I read that all souls had been created at one time. Some, in quest of spiritual growth, got involved in negative activities. So God created human bodies for those souls to inhabit. He created karma so souls could work off the evil they'd done in previous lives.

How quickly souls worked off negative karma and advanced to higher spirit planes depended totally on their own choices—perhaps in only a few lives, maybe in many. But even if they made wrong choices and stacked up more negative karma, they'd only have to live more physical lives on this earth to learn the lessons necessary to live in higher spirit planes. All would get as many opportunities as they needed to balance their karma. There would be no torture in hell for those who happened to make some "wrong" decisions. Just more chances to learn.

The longer I thought about that, the more sense it made. The Bible said God was love. I hadn't been able to think of God as loving since I'd been old enough to start asking questions, since I'd read more than just the few carefully selected Bible stories churches tell children. Maybe adding this new spiritual information to the Bible was the answer.

More than questions haunted me as I worked evenings in the radio studio in the mortuary. Was I alone? Sometimes the hair on the back of my neck suddenly stood on end and goose bumps popped up all over my arms. An eerie sensation would come over me—an electric feeling. *Are souls of the recently departed hanging around?* I wondered. *Are they looking over my shoulder?*

"So what happens to the soul when a person dies?" I asked one night at class.

"Generally, the soul simply slips out of the body," the teacher explained. "They feel great. Lots of mental acuity." He smiled, looked up and off into the distance, and lifted his arms in a gentle, free-swinging arc. "A feeling of being free-ee-ee." A moment later he looked back at me and continued. "After the souls leave their bodies, they can stay around to observe if they choose. They can watch their death, the funeral, the burial, the family matters. Or they can go right on to the spiritual plane they're assigned. It's their choice."

"But does the soul go on to another plane or another life immediately?" I asked.

"Some do and some don't. Each soul chooses. At times, a soul needs rest. They may sleep for awhile, sometimes many years, before they move on. The next step is to view their life and see where they progressed and where they digressed. After that, they request when they'll reincarnate or go on to another plane."

A middle-aged woman a few seats from me noted, "You said, '*Generally,* the soul simply slips out of the body.' Are there exceptions?"

"Yes, sometimes," the teacher answered. "When there's a traumatic death, it sometimes creates havoc for that soul. Such a soul might feel *jerked* out of the body when it wasn't ready. Or yanked out of the body against its will. The soul can be angry. Sometimes it feels its life was incomplete, and it forcibly takes over a new baby's body out of turn, keeping out the other soul that had been scheduled for it. That will probably become an angry child, then an angry adult.

"And sometimes, after death," the teacher continued, "a soul is just confused. The confused souls may be the ghosts that inhabit structures or areas where they used to live. Other times they don't understand that they are dead and they try to talk to people. When their family and friends ignore them, such souls get all the more confused. In those situations, the attending souls treat them patiently, knowing that eventually—maybe years, maybe centuries—the soul will understand what's happening and go on to the proper plane."

The more I learned about reincarnation, the more excited I got. It gave the most logical explanation for humanity's origin and destiny that I'd heard anyplace—far more logical, it seemed to me, than either evolution or any of the churches I'd gone to. It portrayed a loving God—a God who let you have as many chances as you needed to gain spiritual maturity. I felt like shouting my joy from the housetops.

At home, I faithfully practiced self-hypnosis and meditation. At work, eerie sensations continued. Whenever it happened, I wondered, *What kinds of persons arrived at the mortuary today? Are they trying to communicate with me?*

At class, I experienced other regressions to different former lives. In one, I was a suntanned, barefoot boy in a prairie log cabin. The door flew open and a woman carrying two large pails full of milk stepped inside. The woman was obviously my mother. The instant I saw her, immediately to her right I saw a superimposed picture of a former girlfriend of mine in this life—one whom I'd almost married.

A strange feeling washed over me—I'd almost married my mother from a previous life. I'd read that such things are common, that it centers around karma—the law that says you reap what you sow. During their lives, friends, relatives, or marriage partners create circumstances that need to be paid for in a subsequent life. If, for example, I was unfaithful to my wife in a former life, during another life, we might be married again and she be unfaithful to me—only I might be the woman and she might be the man. Or if someone killed me in another life, in this life I might get to kill them.

As much as I enjoyed my new spirituality, one disappointment hung over me—nothing had explained the fall I'd experienced in vision as an infant and then again in my first regression. I couldn't bear to regress back to it—what if it didn't end before I hit the ground? What if I didn't die instantly? What if it took me through extreme pain? Surely there had to be another way to find out.

The terror of the experience and the questions that haunted me prodded me to visit a psychic one afternoon. She closed her eyes and fingered a crystal. After several minutes, she frowned. Eyes still closed, she clenched both hands around the crystal and raised them upward into a beam of sunlight.

A moment later she rested her hands on the table again and opened her eyes. She looked me in the eye. "All I can see is . . ." She cleared her throat. ". . . you are going to die at age thirty from a fall."

"Die?" I questioned. "At thirty?" I swallowed hard. "From a fall?"

She stared intently at the crystal for a long moment. "That's what I see," she concluded.

I left in a daze. *Die? From a fall? Could that have been what the vision when I was a child was about?* The terror of the fall filled me again.

The questions raced faster around the track of my mind than cars at the Indy 500. *Should I go to another psychic to confirm or disprove her prediction?*

Two evenings later at the self-hypnosis class, the instructor taught us how to use a pendulum to get answers "from deep within your soul."

But how could something so simple work? As I drove home, I thought back on the other spiritual skills he'd taught in class. *I've tried them. They've worked! Every single one!* "Finally!" I fairly shouted, giving a thumbs up. "This is what I've been looking for. A way to get specific answers!"

As soon as I arrived home, I assembled the needed supplies and sat at the table. I positioned myself as instructed and asked, "Which direction means 'Yes' for me?"

The key immediately swung away from me, then back, forward, back.

Shivers ran down my spine. *Had I moved?*

I held the string tightly with my right hand and grasped my right hand with my left, steadying my elbows carefully. When the key hung perfectly still, I asked, "Which direction means 'I don't know' for me?"

The key swung to the left in a wide circle.

I know I didn't move. Is there something to this? Then the thought struck—*Ask a different question while it's still swinging.*

"Which direction means 'I won't tell you'?"

Instantly, without continuing its natural arc, the key died in dead center. Not a wisp of movement.

"Which direction means 'No'?"

The key swung a wide left-right arc.

Chills chased each other up and down my spine. *It works! Just like he said!* But for some reason, it felt eerie. *Should I be doing this?* I wondered. *Why is my heart pounding?*

Remembering the counsel of the class leader about praying for protection, I bowed my head. "God, please protect me from any evil spirit influence."

I opened my eyes. The strange, uncomfortable feeling in the pit of my stomach remained. *Shall I ask about the fall?* In the silence I felt like a barbell with 400-pound weights dropped across my shoulders. *Shall I?*

Chapter Four

"Am I Going to Die at Thirty?"

My voice quavered when I finally spoke into the silence. "Am I going to die at thirty from a fall?"

Instantly, the pendulum swung in a wide arc—forward, back, forward, back, forward, back . . . yes . . . yes . . . yes . . .

It slowed nearly to a stop. "Are you sure?"

Instantly it swung wide again—forward, back, forward, back . . . yes . . . yes . . .

I sat there numb. The pendulum had worked exactly as the class instructor had said it would. And it had confirmed my premature demise.

A jumble of everything I'd heard about death rumbled through my mind. I concentrated on the new information I'd been learning.

Since I know in advance, there's no need to fear. My soul won't be surprised. It will simply slip from this body and go on to a plane where

"Am I Going to Die at Thirty?"

I can sort things out and evaluate where and how I need to grow in my next life to get things right.

Fearing the terror of falling, I meditated. *Was what I experienced as a toddler what I had to look forward to when I was thirty? But I was a child. Wasn't that fall from a former life?*

Thinking that the childhood fall was past and that the other fall was several years off comforted me until I wondered, *Did I deal wrongly with the fall in my former life? Do I have to fall again because of karmic debt? How can I be sure I'm ready for it this time?*

The falling situations needled me at times. *Worrying won't delay my demise,* I reasoned. *I have seven years to live. I may as well make the most of them.*

But how? Los Angeles was full of *professional* radio announcers. As a beginner, I couldn't land any better radio job than the part-time one at the automated adult easy listening station. Since I hardly spoke over the air, I wasn't getting much experience that would move me into bigger and better jobs.

I'd met Susan, a beautiful, petite blonde, while in broadcasting school. She came to California to be near me and soon caught my enthusiasm about reincarnation. When we talked marriage, I warned her about my predicted death at thirty. She shook her head. "Maybe it's not for sure. I'll wait and see."

"What other kind of work could you enjoy?" she asked one evening over dinner.

Just the thought of leaving radio sent waves of nausea through me. The reaction surprised me. I thought about previous jobs. "I haven't really liked anything I've done until now. Only went to work to keep eating. Used every excuse I could think up to skip a day." I grinned. "Yeah, body surfing always cured what ailed me when I called in sick!"

She grinned and raised an eyebrow. "I can believe that, the way you love the beach."

"Hm-m-m, I've been in radio nine months now. I love going to work! Haven't missed a single day. Haven't even wanted to."

"That tell you anything?" she asked.

"I guess the question is, do I live where I want to live or do I work at a job I enjoy?"

At home, I asked the pendulum, "Shall I stay in radio?" It swung a deep forward-back arc—yes.

Susan's parents urged us to come to Ohio. We packed our belongings. I landed a job at a small station in Oxford, just outside Cincinnati, and moved into an apartment in an old building that used to be a church. It was the closest I'd been to a church in several years.

Susan and most everyone else thought I was crazy to consider the seven-days-a-week job. But the general manager shrugged off such concerns. "Ah-h-h," he said when he interviewed me, "since you'll only be working a six-hour air shift on Saturday and Sunday, that'll be almost like having those days off." And I had checked the job with a pendulum. It was right. I tackled it with the enthusiasm of a beginner who planned to make it to the top of the radio world in short order.

I loved the job. I immersed myself in accomplishing every aspect of it as perfectly as possible. As news director, I wrote and read the early morning newscasts. Late mornings I traipsed the community selling advertising. I disc jockeyed from 1:00 to 7:00 every afternoon. After that, I'd record commercials then go home about eight or nine and collapse into bed.

When I had a few moments of energy left, I read radio trade journals cover to cover. I especially enjoyed interviews with successful programmers. Could that be the niche I ought to work toward?

Working in radio excited me so much I hardly noticed the wages and schedule—eighty dollars a week, eighty hours a week, and seven days a week. After eight months on the job, the company splurged and gave me one day off—the day *after* Susan's and my wedding.

A few weeks later the manager called me into his office. "Jay, you know we've been struggling financially. We just can't keep going as we are. We've got to eliminate a salary."

My throat went dry.

"We've got to let you go. You've done us a fine job. We don't want to do it. But we just don't have any choice."

I sighed.

"But don't worry about eating and paying the rent. I have a friend who's a building contractor. I called him and he needs a hand. He told me to tell you that, on my recommendation, you're hired." He inhaled deeply. "I'm giving you two weeks notice now. You can start with him two weeks from tomorrow."

My thoughts swirled. Finally I found words. "Thank you for finding me work. I really appreciate it." I sighed and shook my head. "But I can't do that. I love radio. It's got its teeth in me and isn't about to let go."

"I'm with you, Jay. I don't blame you a bit. And you can count on me for a good reference. You've worked really hard for us. You've done a super job. I wouldn't let you go if there was any way I could keep you."

It didn't take long around radio to figure out I'd need to move to bigger stations and more responsibility if I wanted a decent wage. But no large and popular station would hire me with my limited experience. I decided that, in the six years I'd have, I'd work toward repeatedly moving to slightly larger stations. Hopefully, I'd work into the big time.

My next move was to New Castle, Indiana. My daughter Jodi was born there. When I held her for the first time, my heart melted.

Falling for a Lie

I looked at her tiny face and wondered, *Have I known you before in a past life? Or are you someone new I've had no karmic experience with?*

Even before Jodi was born, Susan and I began grating on each other's nerves. The rumblings at home added to the pressures at work were discouraging. *But I can make it,* I told myself. *I only have a few years.* I didn't fear death, only the pain I might experience just before it. Death might even be a relief. Besides, I was eager to learn if I had been responding properly to my karmic debts. My only frustration with dying young was leaving my daughter. *But before her soul accepted this body,* I reminded myself, *it knew her father would die at thirty. It chose this situation because it would provide opportunity for needed spiritual growth.*

I was offered a job doing the midday show at the most popular station in Muncie—WERK. Maybe the change would be good for Susan and me.

As with most decisions, I asked the pendulum. "Should I take it?"

It swung forward and back—yes.

The announcer I replaced on the 10:00 a.m. to 2:00 p.m. show had been extremely popular. Early my first afternoon on the job, when I slipped out of the studio to get a drink of water, I overheard someone sigh and say, "No one will ever take Mark's place. Everyone in town loved him."

I gulped. *They weren't criticizing me,* I tried to convince myself. I took a deep breath. *No, I can't take Mark's place. But,* I vowed, *I'll carve a niche of my own.*

Mark had hosted a talk show at 10:00 every morning. It was mostly a "feel good" type program. When a caller complained about a pothole in front of their house, Mark would commiserate, then give them the name and telephone number of the city official to contact. When a listener made a controversial statement, Mark neither agreed nor took issue. It was an open forum—every subject and every view was wonderful. As the talk show host, Mark provided opportunity for listeners to state their opinions, but he remained impartial. Thus, he remained popular with people of varying persuasions.

I continued his format. "Good morning, Muncie. What are you thinking this morning? The Hotline is ready to take your call."

Sometimes the phone lines were busy. Other days it seemed we couldn't buy a call. What does a talk show host do when no one telephones? Hemming and hawing over radio doesn't increase the listening audience.

The first change I made was to choose a "topic of the day." "Good morning, Muncie. This is The Hotline. The topic this morning is city parks. What city park do you use most? Are the parks maintained adequately? What changes would you like to see?"

Some days the phone lines lighted up before I finished the introduction. Our discussions wandered from potholed streets to school busing to women's liberation. It didn't take long to figure out that the more controversial the topic, the more calls came in. Before long I began stating a controversial opinion up front—sometimes my own opinion, sometimes only stated as such, but always designed to pique listener interest. The Hotline's audience and popularity grew.

Though I tried to plan the topic ahead, one morning when I arrived at the station I still didn't have the slightest idea what topic to discuss on The Hotline in twenty minutes. I desperately scanned the newspaper. Nothing caught my attention in the first three sections.

Suddenly a thought crossed my mind. I lowered the paper and stared at the blank wall.

Falling for a Lie

No way! I love my job. I love Muncie. I'm not ready to be run out of town!

I picked up the paper again. *The ads aren't going to help.* I leafed through the pages quickly then looked at the clock again. *Two minutes!* I looked back at the front page. Nothing.

I still didn't know The Hotline topic when I folded myself into the studio chair.

Should I? I wondered.

What choice do I have? I asked myself. *Besides, it's an opportunity to help some people understand.*

My chest felt tight, my throat dry. "Good morning. This is The Hotline. Most Christians believe that we live one life on this earth. If we accept God and Jesus and live according to God's dictates, then we get to spend an eternity of bliss. But, if we don't do exactly what He wants, we spend an eternity in excruciating pain . . . suffering the fires of hell. Does that make sense to you? Is that a loving God?

"On the other hand, there is a philosophy that says that we have more than one life . . . many lives, as a matter of fact. It's called reincarnation. It teaches that everyone has many opportunities through many lives to perfect their souls . . . and *then* we enter heaven.

"What are your thoughts? Is it one life, then eternal happiness in heaven or eternal suffering in hell? Or is it eventual perfection through reincarnation, leading to an eternity of happiness with God in heaven? Call me at The Hotline."

My pulse pounded in my head.

Several times before I'd considered reincarnation as a topic. But I'd always squealed the mental tires getting away from that idea. Just because I was convinced of reincarnation didn't mean the 75,000 people in this midwest town were ready for it. Why take the chance of flying in the face of organized religion?

And now . . . as I launched into the topic I could see a mental image of the front page of tomorrow morning's newspaper—a huge photo of thousands of shouting Muncie citizens surrounding the station waving hundreds of placards that read, "Away With Jay," "Reincarnate Jay Into Unemployment," and "Burn Hotline. " Would tomorrow morning's local headline read "Popular Hotline Host Fired"?

Chapter Five

The Hotline Heats Up

I pulled myself back to the task at hand. "Good morning, you're on The Hotline."

"Good morning. Hey, I can't believe your topic. . . ."

Here it comes! I worried.

"I've been reading about reincarnation. Makes a lot of sense to me. . . ."

The tension in my shoulders eased slightly. I hoped the listeners didn't hear my sigh of relief.

He continued. "Goin' to heaven when you die and livin' happy ever after sounds good. But what if you make some mistakes along the way?" He paused long enough for a breath. "Then you burn forever alongside the neighbor you never got along with here. That'd be hell all right—to have to put up forever with some of the jerks I've known."

At least this day's not a total disaster! Why, now there's only 74,999 to march on the station demanding my hide!

Another caller asked, "So are you saying I lived another life before this one?

"Tell me," I responded, "do you believe that you'll continue to exist in some way after you die? That your soul or spirit will go on?"

"Yes."

"If you'll go on to another life after this one, why couldn't your present life be after a previous life?"

"B-b-but . . ." Her voice trailed off.

I let the silence hang for several seconds. "If there's more than one life, who says there couldn't be several? Maybe many?"

That caller didn't have much more to say.

"But the Bible doesn't talk about reincarnation," a man who called later insisted.

"The Bible was changed to take out all the references to reincarnation," I told him. "Fortunately, a few texts that speak of reincarnation were missed. For instance, if you're familiar with the Bible, you remember the story of Jesus seeing a man who was born blind. And Jesus' disciples asked Him, 'Who sinned to cause this man to be born blind—this man or his parents?' Remember that?"

"Yes."

"How could the blind man have sinned before he was born if he didn't live a previous life?"

Silence.

"Furthermore," I continued, "if the man *hadn't* had a previous life, that would have been a perfect opportunity for Jesus to straighten out their theology. But He didn't."

Another caller: "I *know* I've had previous lives. Through hypnosis I've regressed into several." He described them enthusiastically.

Another: "This is all new to me. What is 'karma'?"

"Karma is the way a soul can work off the bad in its past. If you did something evil in a previous life, you can balance that by having the same thing done to you in your present or future lives. In fact, the Bible supports this. It says, "Whatsoever a man soweth, that shall he also reap."

Next caller: "But I couldn't have lived before. I don't remember it."

"Most people don't consciously remember previous lives. But, deep within, your soul—your conscience—knows all that it has learned in past lives and knows the schedule for this life."

"But *why* can't I remember it?" the caller persisted.

"If the experiences of previous lives were part of your conscious thought, you might do right things for wrong reasons. True goodness means you do positive things and avoid negative behavior because you *are* good, *not* because you want to advance yourself. Reincarnation isn't worried about a superficial list of dos and don'ts. It's concerned with the inner person, the true motives. When your soul truly lives out love and goodness, you'll be ready to advance to a higher plane where every soul is truly good and loving."

One caller argued, "But you're describing reincarnation differently than I read about in . . ."

"No problem," I responded. "It's different things to different people because the spirits who watch over us and our progress know how much we can understand. Perhaps the authors whose works you read have more advanced understanding than I. Perhaps I'm more advanced than they. Disagreeing doesn't mean one's wrong. It just shows the two parties are at different levels of growth."

"But isn't there a standard?" she asked.

"Yes. Advanced spirits know the standard. They communicate to us what we can understand."

By the end of that program, I wanted to shout for joy. I'd found people who appreciated the reassurance that reincarnation brought. And I'd answered every objection that came up—apparently convincingly. All my worry was wasted.

In fact, reincarnation became one of the most popular topics on The Hotline. Some callers were just curious. Some agreed. Some disagreed respectfully. Some lambasted me. And the ones who condemned me the most telephoned with a list of Bible texts. I noticed they never included the ones that said "Love your enemies" or "God is love." I felt sorry for the Christians with their limited understanding of spiritual realities. *Maybe*, I thought, *if I keep discussing reincarnation, they'll learn to love God too.*

Rather than being run out of town for discussing reincarnation, women's rights, racial discrimination, and most any other controversial topic on The Hotline, the talk show ratings inched higher than ever before. Success!

Before long, I couldn't say "Good morning" to a service station attendant or grocery store clerk without them or someone nearby recognizing my voice. Some wanted to run me out of town, but many fans praised me. Even radio professionals congratulated me.

With all this success, why wasn't I happy? What was missing?

I was still no celebrity with my wife. Finally Susan left . . . with our eighteen-month-old Jodi.

As Susan walked down the sidewalk, Jodi faced me from her mother's shoulder. My daughter's eyes got smaller with each step her mother took toward the waiting car. My heart sank to the soles of my shoes. Jodi's little hand waved bye-bye. But my eyes locked on her face. Especially her sad eyes, wide with question. She stared at me. Like she was trying to get a good picture in mind so she wouldn't forget her daddy. My gut wrenched. Her eyes drilled into mine. Her little hand kept waving.

When their car disappeared, I forced myself back inside and collapsed onto the couch. Life had never felt so dark.

Did I divorce Susan in a former life? I wondered. *What awful*

Falling for a Lie

thing could I have done to deserve losing my daughter? She was the sunshine of my life. What horrid thing could she have done in a previous life to deserve to lose her father? Television couldn't hold my attention. I couldn't relax enough to meditate. I was so befuddled I couldn't even form the jumble of thoughts into questions for a pendulum. It didn't matter. I couldn't muster the energy to move from the couch to the table anyway.

Questions multiplied. Answers didn't show up. Evening dragged. Night seemed to last three weeks. Only one thing made any sense at all—my determination to remain a part of my daughter's life.

I dragged myself to work the next morning—life must go on. Days turned to weeks, weeks to months. I treasured the visits with Jodi. Between them, I poured myself all the more into radio. To survive, I focused on my spiritual life.

Unfortunately, the pendulum I'd depended on began adding to my frustration. Repeatedly, it answered significant questions by swinging left in a wide circle or stopping dead center—"I don't know" or "I won't tell you." I got more and more I-don't-know's and I-won't-tell-you's and less and less Yes's and No's.

On The Hotline I occasionally brought up another of my favorite subjects—Charles Lindbergh. I could talk about him all day . . . whether or not I got any calls.

My fascination about Lindbergh had started early. As a child, I spent every hour I could at a seaplane harbor near my home, watching the float planes taxi and take off, circle and splash down. Sometimes I nosed around the mechanics. "Hey, Mister, what ya doin'?" "How come you're doin' that?" "Why'd you twist that?"

"Mister," I asked a charter pilot one afternoon when I was ten, "how much would you charge to take me up for a ride?"

We settled on seven dollars for half an hour. I went home and started hunting odd jobs. A dollar for raking the neighbor's leaves.

Thirty cents here. Fifty cents there. I saved for weeks. Seemed like eons.

Finally I delivered the seven dollars—three dollar bills and a pocketful of change. The moment we climbed into the plane, I felt at home—like I'd flown before. We skimmed the lake at full throttle, then lifted away from the lake. I thrilled while we wandered the sky over streets, parks, and lakes. We even flew over my house. I dreamed of barnstorming with Charles Lindbergh. I didn't want to ever land.

But one plane fascinated me more than all others—Charles Lindbergh's *Spirit of St. Louis*. I read every book the library had about it. Mom and Dad bought me his book, *We*. I read it so much we had to patch the cover.

Even at school, when I was supposed to be studying verbs, prepositions, or multiplication tables, I was more apt to be drawing the *Spirit of St. Louis*. And in the pictures the details were right—license number N-X-211, NYP on the tail, the extra long wings, and *Spirit of St. Louis* written proudly across the side of the cowling.

Through the years, whenever I heard about Charles Lindbergh or Charles Lindbergh, Jr., I felt an odd sense of empathy that puzzled me. Curiosity drove me to read, watch, and listen to everything I could find about them. Maybe someone would call The Hotline with a detail that would help me fit it together.

But reincarnation was the hottest topic. One morning while discussing it again, a caller named Marlene reported, "The weirdest thing happened at our house the other night. It scared us half out of our wits. But now that you're talking about spirits from other planes, I wonder if that could have something to do with it."

"What happened?"

"I needed something in the attic. My neighbor came to visit, so she went up with me to help get it. Just after we'd walked through the door, colored lights started flashing all around us. Some just flashed on, then off again. Others swept around the room—all over the floor and ceiling."

"Just tiny little blips of light?"

"No. Bright lights! So bright they nearly blinded us."

"Any sound?"

She cleared her throat. "Huh-uh. No sound at all. At least I didn't hear any."

"So what did you do?"

"We just stood there. Silent. My heart was pounding. But the lights didn't quit. Finally I caught my breath enough to say, 'Let's get out o' here!' and we backed down the stairs as quickly as we could." She paused. "I was terrified."

"So, have you seen anything unusual since?" I asked.

"No one's been back in the attic!"

"Has there been anything unusual anyplace else in the house?"

"Nothing. And believe me, the way we've been tiptoeing around here and watching for anything weird, we'd have noticed it if there were anything."

Just considering the opportunity Marlene had, my heart beat faster. "If the spirits are trying to talk with you," I suggested, "you might find out wonderful things if you went back up there."

She caught her breath loudly enough that I heard a *whoosh* over my headset. "Not on your life! My neighbor made it plain she's not going up there again. And I'm sure not going up there alone!"

"Do you know anyone that might go with you?" I asked.

"Not a soul. No one I've mentioned it to wants any part of it." She paused briefly. "Hey!" she exclaimed, "Would you?"

Late that afternoon, anticipation filled me as I parked my car in front of a gray house with white shutters. I double-checked the house number and turned off the engine. "God," I whispered, "please let the spirits come. I need some spiritual encouragement!"

Chapter Six

Secrets From the Spirits

"Good afternoon, I'm Jay Christian from The Hotline. You invited me to come look at the lights . . ."

"Yes, yes. Come on in."

Marlene chattered nervously as we headed down a hall. "I'm glad you came. I don't think I'd ever have gone up in the attic again." She led me to a stairway. "After you," she offered with a sheepish grin.

My heart beat faster. I couldn't swallow the lump in my throat. *Maybe I'll get to talk with spirits from another plane*, I thought as I climbed the stairs. *Reincarnation has helped me make some sense out of life, but there's still the two questions that have haunted me since childhood. Maybe they'll have answers!*

The attic door squeaked open into a single, small room with a window on each end. Half a dozen boxes sat along the wall to my left. A couple lamps and a wooden chair with a broken leg stood near the window to my right. The side walls left and right of the door were short. The ceiling peaked in the middle, barely taller than I. I walked several feet down the center, then turned and glanced around the room. Marlene stepped just inside the doorway. We waited in silence for several minutes.

"Where were the lights?" I asked.

"All over. A red one would flash there, then a blue one here. Then a pink light, or white, or green, or orange." She pointed to differing spots all over the attic as she spoke. "Some lights came on, then swept around the room. Others just flashed quickly." She snapped her fingers. "Shorter than that."

"Did they come on one at a time?"

"No, no. Well, I guess a few did. But sometimes there were several lights . . . different colors . . . sweeping all over the attic from different directions. And they were bright!"

"How bright?"

"Nearly blinding. Even brighter than when you're driving straight into the sun."

For half an hour we waited and wondered aloud together about the phenomena. But nothing happened.

We finally descended the stairs. Disappointed, I headed home.

"God," I prayed that night, "Why won't you talk to me? Marlene and her friend must have encountered spirits. And I've read about others' experiences with spirits. I want to grow. I want to make sense out of my life. I want to know about the future so I can be prepared for it. Please send a spirit to teach me."

I pictured a warm, casual conversation with a soul. Day after day I prayed for the experience. A source of wisdom seemed especially important to me since the pendulum was nearly useless. I thought back to my initial instructions in pendulum use: "The pendulum won't answer every question you ask it. It will sometimes refuse to give you an answer. Sometimes, if it knows you can't handle the answer, it will even lie to you."

So, I wondered, *if it answers a preponderance of my questions with "I don't know" or "I won't tell you" and if I can't trust it when it answers some other way, what good is it?*

It's almost like it worked perfectly to begin with but dropped me when I really learned to depend on it.

I gave up on the pendulum and prayed the harder for an opportunity to visit with a spirit.

One afternoon, I stretched out on my bed and took a nap. When I'd half-wakened, I continued to rest on my right side, facing the wall.

Suddenly, a hand grasped my left shoulder and pulled me onto my back. Knowing I was home alone, I shook off the sleepiness and looked up.

Several feet above me and three or four feet to my left, I clearly saw a grandmotherly face. She wore heavily-framed glasses with upswept points at her temples. Curly gray hair framed her smile and kindly eyes. But I could see no body. Just a face.

My hands turned cold and clammy.

She smiled. "You wanted to talk to me?"

"I don't know you!" I responded coldly. "Go away!"

Her smooth, gentle voice spoke again. "What would you like to know?"

Even though her eyes exuded understanding, terror pulsed through me and pounded in my head. I felt frozen. Finally, words escaped again past the lump in my throat. "Go away! I don't know you!"

"I'll wait a few minutes in case you change your mind."

She hung around, literally, for several minutes. All her expressions and mannerisms indicated she was a friendly soul, but terror still filled me. "Leave! Please leave!" I gasped.

Falling for a Lie

She faded . . . slowly.

Several minutes later my heart slowed and quit pounding. I breathed deeply, slowly, trying to relax. When my terror had nearly vanished, my senses returned. *Oh no! This was the answer to my prayer! My chance to find answers. I blew it!*

"Please, God," I begged, "give me another opportunity."

Several weeks later a friend invited me to a séance. "Is this one for real?" I questioned.

"What do you mean, for real?"

"I've heard about séances and, frankly, I'm skeptical."

"Why?"

"I guess . . . I think . . . some of them are . . . phony. Probably some are for real. But I suspect a lot are a sham."

"Well, I thought it was for real when I went," she responded. "You'll just have to come and make up your own mind."

"OK. Let's go. I haven't had any more opportunities to talk with spirits. Maybe God will speak to me through a séance. At the very least, it should be interesting."

We arrived at an old house and went downstairs into the basement. I glanced around the room. There were no windows. Folding chairs were arranged in a semicircle facing a stage in one corner. On the stage sat a chair with a curtain behind it and pillows strewn in front of it. Four trumpets stood near the chair, with their mouthpieces toward the ceiling. These weren't ordinary trumpets. They were straight from the mouthpiece to the flared bell. And they had no finger controls for changing pitch.

"The spirits," my friend explained, "will speak to us through the trumpets."

"But why should I believe anyone really uses the trumpets?" I questioned.

"See how they're standing?"

"Yeah."

"Since the spirits don't have bodies, they use the trumpets as their voice boxes. They will levitate the trumpets, talk through them, then leave them lying strewn about the floor so we can know they have indeed been used by spirits."

Several others came in and sat down in the semicircle also.

"Oh, by the way," my friend added, "sometimes during the séance a spirit will actually come into the room so we can see it. When that happens, it's a tiny light that flits about the room, like . . . well . . . like Tinkerbell."

Page 45

A middle-aged woman entered. My friend caught her attention. "Come meet my friend, Jay."

She offered her hand. "Glad to have you here, Jay." We chatted briefly before she moved to the stage and settled into the chair. When she nodded, a young man flipped the light switch and darkness filled the room. Darkness so dark that you felt it. *As dark as this is*, I thought, *anyone could do anything and no one could see it happen.*

"God," the woman began, "I ask for your protection from evil spirits that might harm or mislead, and I ask your blessing on each of us. Amen."

Silence filled the blackness. Then a tiny light flitted about the room. Like a firefly whose light didn't go out. Indeed, like Tinkerbell, the tiny fairy of Disney fame. It floated and flitted about for what seemed like several minutes. Then it disappeared as suddenly as it had appeared.

The leader spoke again. "I see Bob. He died when he was seventy-seven. Does anyone know a Bob?"

"Yes," an elderly woman answered eagerly.

"Bob, do you know this lady?" She paused. "Irene, it is your husband. Bob, do you have words for Irene?" Silence again. "Irene," the woman said, "Bob says life is great where he is. He is taking the opportunity to learn about things he did in his life here. He's planning out the process of karma so he can take the best advantage of everything he's learned."

The widow asked a series of questions about family and financial decisions, and the medium passed on his suggestions. "Bob says," the medium concluded, "that if you follow everything he told you tonight, your finances will improve greatly."

"Oh, thank you," the widow responded. "I miss him so much. But it helps me tremendously to be able to hear from him."

There was silence again for a minute. Then the medium said, "I see a young woman. She was killed in a car crash. . . ."

A woman to my right caught her breath.

"Her name is . . . uh . . . Joanne."

"It's my daughter!" a woman gasped.

My head swam as different souls sent messages through the medium to different individuals. In the middle of one, a thought struck me—*Several years have gone by. If I get a chance, I'll ask if the spirits see a fall in my future.*

Eventually the medium lapsed into silence again. Then a deeper voice spoke . . . from the woman in the chair. With a strong accent, it said, "I am Chief Running River. I left my body two of your centuries ago and have gained much wisdom. I have come to you before. I come again to give you guidance in your search for truth."

The room was hushed while he spoke. Finally, his mellow voice concluded, "Live good lives. It's more important now than it ever has been before that you create little or no negative karma. Soon the earth will shift on its axis. There will be such widespread destruction that many people will die. With a much smaller population, far fewer babies will be born. So, until the world has regenerated its population, it will be much harder, much slower to work off negative karma and move on to higher planes.

"The souls of your ancestors are waiting to be reunited with you," he continued. "Some may even be your guardian angels in this life. They will help you to keep your 'teepees' in order so you can come quickly to advanced planes."

After a long silence, he spoke again. "I must go now. Stay open to the spirits. Listen for their voices. Always follow their advice."

The medium broke the hush in the room with a sigh, then spoke again in her own voice. "The spirits say it is time to speak through the trumpets. A spirit will come, pick up a trumpet, and talk through it," she explained for us newcomers. "The trumpets are just another way for us to hear the wisdom of other souls on various topics."

The medium called up spirit guides of three other individuals. The voices that spoke through the trumpets had a high, tinny sound. They were garbled—hard to understand, but not impossible.

Indeed this does seem like it's for real, I thought. *There's been information and guiding suggestions that, surely, not just anyone would know.*

But the intense darkness kept intriguing me. My eyes had had more than ample time to adjust. I held up one hand just a couple inches in front of my face. I still couldn't see my hand, let alone anything else.

Then the medium said it was my turn. *We'll see,* I thought, not totally believing or disbelieving.

"Will Jay's spirit guide please come to talk with him through a trumpet?" the medium asked.

A burst of electricity jolted through me. "Go ahead, Jay," she said. "What questions do you have for your spirit guide?"

"First," I said, "would you just speak so I can hear your voice?"

An eerie, thin voice from a trumpet said, "Ja-a-a-a-ay, I'm he-ee-ee-ere."

Falling for a Lie

If this is truly my own spirit guide who has been with me from birth, I thought, *he'll know my real name as well as my radio name.* "Isn't there something else you want to call me other than Jay?"

The thin, eerie voice stuttered, "Uh-h-h-h . . ."

"Don't test it!" the medium broke in. "You're not supposed to test it! It upsets the spirits greatly!"

Chapter Seven

Power Run Amok

Irritation filled the medium's voice. "The spirits won't talk to you if you don't believe who they are!"

"Fine," I said. "Any spirit guide of mine who doesn't even know my real name probably couldn't tell me much of value anyway."

The assistant cleared his throat. "The physical demands of conducting these sessions are very draining. It's time to end."

The medium prayed, then meditated as dim lights came on. The assistant slowly turned the lights brighter. The medium straightened in her chair and talked with various attendees.

"This is so-o-o wonderful!" the elderly woman's enthusiasm bubbled over loudly. "I'm so-o-o glad I can keep in touch with my husband! His advice helps me so-o-o much!"

I overheard a middle-aged man say, "My business training and experience sure didn't prepare me to pull myself out of the financial mess I'm in. Sure, it'll be high interest, but I'm going tomorrow morning to see about getting the loan my spirit guide suggested.

49

Falling for a Lie

Man, will I be glad to get my life turned around!"

Everyone else seemed absorbed in their own experience. I was shocked that no one else seemed even slightly concerned about my "spirit guide" not knowing my name. "In my opinion," I told my friend as I started the car, "that was a bunch of malarkey."

"But what about the other voices? What about that woman who makes it through life because she can hear from her husband?"

"There may be something to séances held where the participants can see what's going on, but the intense darkness is crazy. Doesn't take much of an actor to fake different voices. Why the total darkness, anyway?"

"When it's dark, there are less distractions. It's easier to meditate."

"Well, you can go back as often as you like, but I'm not wasting my time. It was nothing but a show."

So-o-o, where do I look?

The highlight of my life was the monthly weekend visits with Jodi. Her little-girl playfulness relaxed me. And since she'd only have a daddy till she was six, I treasured each opportunity to teach her what I had learned.

I enjoyed work in Muncie. Hosting the talk show kept life challenging and interesting. As production director, I broadened my experience in producing commercials and organizing things so that each commercial was taped by the appropriate person and in the studio before its time to play. With The Hotline and my mid-day music show, people all over town recognized my voice. I delighted in the variety of people who said "I love your show!"

But prestige wasn't as gratifying as I'd hoped. My spiritual quest deepened. By the time I accepted a position with WAMS in Wilmington, Delaware, I didn't even have to induce hypnosis to glimpse other lives. Visions came off and on—something like daydreams, but much more vivid.

As music director and afternoon drive announcer at WAMS, I met a number of recording artists. Some excelled in self. Others seemed genuinely interested in local events and people. Barry Manilow, for one. He had served as Bette Midler's music director and had wowed her fans with his mid-show performance. Eventually, he went out on his own. As music director at WAMS, I and five other radio personalities were invited to Philadelphia to attend one of his first concerts and then to meet him in his dressing room backstage. He was every bit as personable one-on-one as he was on stage. When his first song "Mandy" was released several weeks later, we started playing it immediately.

A year later, Barry Manilow was back in Philadelphia at a much larger theater. He'd had a blockbuster year—articles galore were written about him, he faced radio and TV interviews constantly, and "Mandy" had just hit Number One in the nation on the Billboard "Hot 100" music chart. With his exploding popularity, instead of a half-dozen radio invitees, several hundred people jammed into a much larger dressing room. When I stopped to shake the singer's hand, he smiled and said, "How's it going at WAMS, Jay?"

I couldn't believe my ears. Had I been from a major station, I probably would have been cynical. But, being from a small station that couldn't do much to advance his career, I was amazed!

One afternoon the Pointer Sisters were scheduled to stop at our station. I expected them to come in, do a few minutes on air, record a few station promotional announcements, jump into their limo, and leave. Fifteen minutes, tops.

So much for expectations. After the interview, they stayed all afternoon. They helped me do my show. They talked to people on the phone. They hung around the station doing whatever came to mind. They filled the station with fun, friendliness, and humor.

Falling for a Lie

It didn't take long to see there was as wide a variety in the characters of celebrities as in the rest of the world's population. And it felt good to have respectable celebrities showing me respect.

One afternoon during my show, the secretary cracked open the studio door. "There's a lady out here who won a record in your contest."

"Tell her I'll be there to get it as soon as I start the next song."

Minutes later when I turned the corner, I did a double take. An incredibly beautiful woman smiled up at me pleasantly. *Whoa! She listens to me?*

I gathered my wits, led her to my office, thanked her for listening, gave her the record, and shook my head as she left. A couple days later she called with a request. Come to find out, she had been a regular caller to request songs while I was on the air. But now I placed that name and voice with a mental image of a lady with long black hair, olive skin, brown eyes that danced, and a smile that could warm a cold day.

Eventually, I asked Maria to dinner. She was a real head-turner. As we got better acquainted, I found she was more than beautiful. She was also fun and friendly. One evening on the phone, she said, "The other day on the radio you mentioned karma on your show. Do you believe in karma?"

"Yes, matter of fact, I do," I responded, thinking I may have just lost a listener and a friend.

"You believe in reincarnation?"

"Yes, I believe in it and look forward to learning and growing as rapidly as I can. Why do you ask?"

"Well, I believe in it too. And I just really appreciate knowing others who have grown beyond tradition and embraced advanced spiritual concepts."

Our shared belief in reincarnation drew us together. As I became acquainted with Maria, I repeatedly saw a vision of the two of us meeting in front of a white stone building that looked like it was of ancient Greek or Roman architecture. We met to talk but were always very quiet about it. I sensed it was some sort of clandestine meeting.

"Maria," I said one evening, "I keep seeing a vision of us meeting together."

She smiled. "Do we by any chance meet in front of a white stone building?"

My eyes widened. "Yes."

"And stairs on either side of the building meet at the top forming a small porch in front of a door? And small recessed windows flank the door on left and right?"

My mouth dropped open. "Yes."

"And we both wear white, except your tunic has a dark tie around the waist?"

"Maria, I can't believe it! That's exactly what I saw. How'd you know?"

"I've seen it too," she said matter-of-factly. "We were together in Greece a long time ago in former lives."

I just sat there shaking my head.

Then she asked, "Do you remember ever being a sailor?"

"Perish the thought!" I grimaced. "I get seasick just thinking about the ocean!"

"But have you ever seen anything in a vision that would even suggest life as a sailor?"

"Not in this life or any other," I assured her. "One trip to Korea in a troop transport ship with my head hanging over the railing is more than enough ocean travel for many lives!"

"Well, my dear, even if you've not seen it yet," Maria assured me, "you were a sailor in another lifetime. I was your girl in the home port and whenever you returned, we spent most of our time together."

"O-o-o-K." I shuddered at the thought.

"Yes, I've even seen you and me together by a scraggly tree on top of a big cliff of white rocks overlooking water. I'm not positive, but I think we were likely on the white cliffs of Dover, England.

"OK, OK. I'm glad it was a *former* lifetime! And I certainly hope I don't have any karma to work off on an ocean!"

Maria laughed at my dismay.

"By the way," I said, "a while back you mentioned that you used to have greater psychic powers than you do now."

Maria's face blanched.

I pressed on. "Why do you think you lost the power?"

She shivered. "I didn't lose it, exactly. I suppress it."

"Why?"

"Because . . ." Maria shuddered as her voice trailed off. Her expression turned dark as a thundercloud. "Never mind. I haven't told a soul."

"It's OK. You can trust me with it."

"It scares me."

"Why?"

"I don't want to be responsible for it."

"What do you mean?" I urged her on.

"Well, I didn't used to realize the power that was involved." She stared out the window. "Then a friend of mine was dating a real jerk. One evening Mike beat her up because dinner wasn't ready when he arrived. No questions. Just beat her up. Broke her arm and bloodied and bruised her all over. The next afternoon she dropped by and we talked a while. I got so angry I said, 'I wish he were dead!'

"The words were barely out of my mouth when my friend looked at her watch and jumped up. 'Ouch!' She winced when she bumped the cast on her arm against the table. 'Hey, it's 3:25. I've got an appointment at 3:30.'

"She took off. A couple hours later she telephoned. 'Have you heard the news?'

"'No,' I said. 'Why?'

"'Mike was killed in a car accident.'

"The news that night said witnesses saw the car swerve off the road and hit a tree at 3:25 p.m. It was daylight. The road was dry. There weren't any cars near enough to cause a problem. There was no apparent reason. And he was killed instantly."

She sighed. "At 3:25 I said 'I wish he were dead.' At the same moment, he died." She looked down at her feet, then closed her eyes and shook her head. "I feel responsible for his death."

Chapter Eight

Thirty

Maria and I shared a spiritual bond that neither of us had enjoyed with any other. Our closeness, even with Maria knowing me so well, meant the world to me. Especially when work started getting stressful again.

The situation felt too familiar. When I looked back, a pattern emerged. I would arrive at a new station with high hopes. I'd do the best job I could and I'd get along fine for awhile. I'd gain the respect of some, but, sooner or later, a co-worker or several would get disgruntled and make it their job to make mine difficult. Whether I resigned or got fired, I'd go to a new job with high hopes and the cycle would start over. What was I doing wrong?

Whatever, here I go again.

Toward the end of one interview that seemed to be going well, the manager looked me straight in the eye and said, "I'm not interested in a fly-by-nighter for this position. I want someone who's going to commit to our station and be popular with our listeners for some time." He looked down at my resumé.

I wasted a trip here, I thought.

"Yeah, every place you've been, you've stayed a year . . . a year and a half. That's what I like—commitment."

Puzzling over his comment later, I thought back on the people I'd worked with, the radio personalities I'd talked with, the radio trade journals I'd read. Announcers or programmers who stayed very long in any position were a miniscule minority. I realized for the first time what a volatile profession I'd chosen.

Volatile or not, I loved radio. Before long I accepted the job of music director at Baltimore, Maryland. It seemed like a station and job I could enjoy.

Shortly after I arrived, management ordered a new promotional tool—a thirty-foot white balloon shaped like a blimp. The big blue capital Q on the nose and either side would, hopefully, make people think of Q-104, as we called our station. Its premiere appearance would be atop a fourteen story hotel just off the Beltway.

As soon as the balloon arrived, the general manager scheduled a crew to set it up late the next afternoon. On the roof we reviewed the plan—two guys would inflate the balloon while I held the nose steady and three others held the larger rear section. It would have been a piece of cake on a nice day.

Unfortunately, as I was tying the front end down, the breeze gusted into a gale. I needed the hands of two men and the strength of five to hold the front steady while I fastened it. "Whew," I sighed when I finished. My arms felt weak. I glanced across to the others. They looked like they were managing fine. My work done, I got curious. *Fourteen stories up looks tall. What does fourteen stories down look like?*

I walked to the edge of the roof. The cars below looked like the matchbox cars kids collected. The people bustling to and from the hotel looked like so many giant ants scurrying about their hill.

I'd enjoyed the view only a moment when an authoritative voice that sounded like it came from about two feet behind my right ear commanded, "GET DOWN!"

I didn't ask questions or turn to see who spoke. Instantaneously, I dropped to my knees. I planted my left knee against the two-foot wall around the perimeter of the roof. I gripped the top of the wall like my life depended on it.

The instant I anchored myself, something hit me hard in the middle of the back. So hard that it knocked the air out of me. So hard that my chest and head jerked over the wall, out over fourteen stories of space with hard pavement at the bottom.

The blood drained from my face. I jumped backward, away from the wall. My legs felt like boiled spaghetti. My hands trembled.

Wind whistled over the roof as another gust hit. I glanced around. Everyone else was fighting to hold the rear of the balloon and pull it back toward the tie-down ring. The tie at the rear had apparently come loose and the wind had whipped the balloon into my back.

I checked my tie-down knots—they were holding—and rushed to the back of the balloon.

"Jay! Help us!" one of the crew yelled when he saw me.

Another gust hit, nearly tearing the balloon away from the crew again. I grabbed a handhold and fought along with the rest.

By the time the balloon was secured, every person there looked like they'd fought with a heavyweight boxer and lost. We caught our breath in gasps.

We double-checked and triple-checked the knots and stayed by to make sure no gust would launch the balloon into the next state.

"By the way," I asked between gasps, "who warned me?"

Each one scrunched his nose or raised an eyebrow. "What?" several chorused almost together.

"Who warned me to get down when the balloon broke loose?"

They looked at each other and shrugged their shoulders. "We were all busy back here," one said. "Nobody warned you."

That evening I telephoned Maria.

"Jay, are you OK?" she asked as soon as she heard my voice.

"Yes, fine. Why?"

"Well . . . you're thirty. And today . . . I had a premonition."

I told her the story.

"This was the predicted fall!" she assured me. "I'm positive!"

"But why?" I asked. "Why would the spirits tell me I was going to die at thirty from a fall and then warn me the last minute so I wouldn't?"

"Maybe," she suggested, "because you're destined for something big. Perhaps you've handled karma so well that now you're going to do something really worthwhile in this world."

"Well, whatever, I have some thinking to do. I hadn't planned life beyond thirty."

I prayed: "God, what do I do now?" I read. Nothing gave me direction. I meditated. No images or ideas came. Months went by without a single vision. A white fog of uncertainty settled around me: I slept, ate, went to work. But I couldn't see into the fog that covered tomorrow.

Have I done something so negative the spirits won't even communicate with me? I wondered. *That doesn't make sense! If I'd been stacking up more negative karma, no spirit would have protected me from falling off the hotel roof. What's the purpose in my life? What am I supposed to be doing?*

Amidst the spiritual silence, I finally decided I may as well continue with my pre-thirty goals—personally, treat people right so I

Falling for a Lie

can move to higher planes as quickly as possible and, professionally, move to bigger and better stations and work toward programming and management.

One evening a TV movie about the kidnapping of Charles Lindbergh, Jr. played. With my Lindbergh fascination, I settled in to watch it.

Minutes into the movie I plopped cross-legged onto the floor three feet in front of the TV, a large pop and full bag of chocolate chip cookies on the floor beside me. As the movie progressed, tightness gripped my chest. Before long I was leaning forward watching every move, listening closely for every word. Anxiety overcame me. I was reacting with the terror I'd felt when I experienced falling during regression.

When the movie showed the actor that played the accused kidnapper—Bruno Richard Hauptman, I muttered, "He didn't do it! They've got the wrong man!"

What is wrong with me, I wondered. *Why do I care? It's history.*

But reasoning with myself didn't curb the extreme emotion that had overcome me. My palms sweat. My heart pounded. I felt an overwhelming sense that a horrible injustice was being done, like somebody had to stop it. "It's not him!" I exclaimed over and over. "They've got the wrong man!"

But the movie played on. My muscles tensed the tighter. Even though I hated what I saw, I couldn't force my body off the floor or unglue my eyes from the screen. Tears flowed down my cheeks. I couldn't believe it. I never cried. But I was crying. Part of the time I rocked back and forth. "He didn't do it!" I shouted.

By the end of the movie, I hadn't touched the pop or my favorite cookies. I forced myself to my feet, then collapsed onto the bed, totally exhausted.

What in the world is going on? Why am I so upset? I couldn't figure out why the extreme emotion had engulfed me. For days afterward, I couldn't shake the sense of injustice. Nor could I keep myself from waking at night shouting, "He didn't do it!"

"Please, God," I prayed, "please send answers. Life isn't making sense."

Months dragged by. I checked out a job in Muscle Shoals, Alabama. It met my number-one criteria for every job—within a day's driving distance of my daughter, Jodi. And it was in programming. I had read everything I could about programming. I'd watched and evaluated the whats and whys of the effectiveness of every program director I had worked with. WLAY was my chance to give it a try, even if it was only as assistant program director. I was also mid-day announcer and music director.

But, despite accolades related to work, I felt frustrated by the lack of spiritual contact. "God," I prayed, "What's going on? You kept me alive. Why? What am I supposed to be doing?"

Through the silent months that followed, an uncanny identification with Charles Lindbergh and his family kept resurfacing—images from my earliest childhood reading, my charter flight, the movie about the baby's kidnapping. Sometimes the terror of my childhood "fall" squeezed in among the Lindbergh thoughts.

Maria and I talked on the phone frequently. But even she, with her spiritual sensitivity, couldn't make sense out of the jumble of my life.

One evening, after a particularly long and trying day at work, I parked my new burgundy Corvette in the garage, closed and latched the heavy wooden doors, and trudged up the steps to my second-story apartment directly above the ground-level garage. I collapsed onto my bed and drifted in and out of an exhausted stupor.

I woke with a start. *Did I set the 'Vette's security system?* Though it was parked directly below my bed, I couldn't pull myself off the

Falling for a Lie

bed to trudge down the steps, check the alarm, and climb back up. I lay there, worrying.

Suddenly, I floated above the living-room floor, through the closed entry door—*through* the door, not the doorway, down the steps, around the side of the garage, through the garage door—through, again, and over to the car. I noted that the alarm activation lock on the left front fender was set. Then, looking through the windshield on the driver's side, I noticed my sunglasses hanging on the rearview mirror. That surprised me since I ordinarily put them in the glove compartment. Assured that the alarm was set, I glided directly up *through* the apartment floor and into my body on the bed.

My eyes opened with a start. *That was too vivid for a dream! Did I actually do it?*

Chapter Nine

Fears and Ratings

Is that what an out-of-body experience is like? I wondered.

First thing the next morning I checked the car. Yes, the alarm was set. And, yes, my sunglasses hung from the mirror, exactly as I'd seen them the night before.

The spirits are still watching out for me, I concluded. *My karma must have just needed for me to work through this time without spirit contact.*

Life looked brighter again. I prayed with more intensity for answers. And then one morning I was in vision again. I saw a toddler standing on the roof of an old building and sensed that it was myself. A door with small glass panes opened into an apartment and I stood on the roof—the apartment's large porch. A woman wearing a long dress and a long apron stood to the left of the door, wringing her hands. Two men with brown, slicked-back hair and brown pin-striped suits stood just outside the door. They glanced about and whispered apprehensively.

Suddenly, I stamped my feet and screamed. As the toddler (me) screamed, words flashed through my adult mind: "My daddy's famous! If you don't let me go, he's going to get you!" Then the toddler (me) turned and ran. At the edge of the roof my little feet kept going. Suddenly, I was falling. Red brick walls and windows with small panes flashed by as I tumbled down . . . down . . . down . . .

Terror filled me. Even in my child brain, I knew I was going to die! I was still free falling with arms and legs flailing when the vision ended.

Terror gripped every muscle in my body. My heart pounded in my head. I closed my eyes and breathed deeply. *Calm down*, I told myself. *Get a grip.*

But besides the terror I'd felt when I saw the vision as a toddler and when I'd experienced my first regression, an added panic gripped. *Could it be? No! Surely not! I don't want it to be!*

"Please give me answers, God," I begged. "I don't want to be the reincarnation of anyone famous. I just want to learn what I need to know to work through my negative karma and move to a higher plane. Please help me make sense out of this!"

No further visions came. The spirits seemed to turn a deaf ear again.

Deeply frustrated with my spiritual life in general and my questions about the fall in particular, I immersed myself in work. Muscle Shoals, Alabama, was one of the biggest song-recording areas in the country. One of the highlights of working there was meeting and interviewing music stars and being invited to sit in on recording sessions.

Mingling with stars boosted my morale . . . usually. But one morning after I'd moved to WHHY in Montgomery, Alabama, my boss handed me a tape recorder and said, "Go out to the clubhouse and interview someone famous."

I headed out to the annual charity Celebrity Golf Tournament. The first person I saw was Pat Boone. As he walked out the club-house door after the interview, I pushed the rewind button to check the tape. But the recorder switched right back off. I pushed play. Silence. Fast forward. Play. Silence.

Oh, no! I blew it big time! A great interview and . . . now what?

I scratched my head. *I could just ignore it. Act like nothing happened and go interview someone else. Should I tell Pat Boone what happened? He could think I was a complete idiot and tell me, "Tough luck. You had your chance."*

I swallowed hard and leaned out the door. "Pat?"

He turned.

"I feel like a real fool, but I failed to push the 'record' button. If you have a few minutes, could we talk again?"

He chuckled. "Sure. No problem."

I made sure the tape recorder was working!

Interview take-two was just as pleasant as the first. Pat Boone answered my questions with flair . . . again. He had a ready smile and positive comments. He seemed genuinely happy. He was to-tally gracious.

Many celebrities, even if they'd tried to be nice, would have betrayed themselves with a roll of their eyes, a grimace, or other body language. I knew Pat Boone claimed to be a Christian and his reputation was as squeaky-clean as his traditional white buck shoes. But he was so gracious. So nonjudgmental. Not like a lot of Chris-tians I'd known.

The lesson in humility didn't seem to hurt my career. A few months later, WHBB in Selma, Alabama, offered me the opera-tions manager position.

Management! I couldn't stand complacency in radio. I hated to

Falling for a Lie

see a job botched when it could be done well with a little dedication to excellence. Here was my chance to make a difference in the profession I loved!

With my eyes focused on perfection, I jumped at the opportunity.

Another fact about Selma interested me—Edgar Cayce had lived there. Through the years since I had attended the self-hypnosis classes, I'd continued reading about him. I joined an Edgar Cayce study group there and thoroughly enjoyed the spiritual fellowship.

While I lived in Selma, Edgar Cayce's personal secretary, Gladys Davis, and Hugh Lynn Cayce, one of Edgar Cayce's sons, came to dedicate a plaque in front of his father's former photography studio. As well as meeting them and covering the dedication on radio, I scheduled a radio interview with Hugh Lynn. For half an hour we promoted reincarnation and associated beliefs. I enjoyed the interview thoroughly.

Hugh Lynn seemed to sense my sincere interest. During his stay in Selma, we met for lunch or breakfast several other times. These times had nothing to do with radio. We simply visited as friends. Hugh Lynn was open and honest, kind and sincere. I reveled in the stories he shared—a number about his parents and some of his own spiritual experiences. Besides the high respect I had for his father, I developed a deep personal bond with Hugh Lynn.

I was tempted to ask him about my visions of a small boy falling off a roof. But would he confirm my fears? I didn't bring them up.

Maria and I treasured our friendship—especially the spiritual fellowship—and the phone calls and trips between Selma and Wilmington threatened to bankrupt us both. We married and she moved to Selma, complete with pet skunk, Sweet Pea. Maria loved animals and animals of all kinds loved her.

Fears and Ratings

When I felt I'd accomplished everything I could at the station in Selma, I started looking elsewhere. Shortly, WDOD Chattanooga offered me the job of program director at an FM station that was partly religious, partly easy listening, and partly anything that anyone would sponsor. The plan was to change it to a rock-and-roll format and challenge the station that was number one—another rock station.

I knew I'd miss Selma and the spiritual stimulation of friends in the study group. But neither Maria's psychic powers nor my own meditation showed me any reason not to accept the job.

As I looked over the situation in Chattanooga, it occurred to me that what they really needed was a country-music station. But I didn't know a thing about country. Besides, I had been hired specifically to put a rock format on the air.

It was hard work—finding all the music we wanted to play, hiring a complete air staff, organizing the sound of the station, and getting it all done in time to meet our target air date. The budget was too small for a lot of advertising. But we worked hard and had a lot of fun. We did everything we could to get attention by word of mouth. Then came ratings.

Radio life revolves around ratings. The announcers want to know their individual ratings. Pride plays a part—it really feels good to know there are a lot of people in the community who listen to your show. But, also, if an announcer's ratings are good, their job is more apt to be secure. Program directors need good ratings to keep their jobs. Sales managers want good ratings so they can sell commercials and their stations can make money. General managers want good ratings for higher salaries, financial success for their stations, and job security. Off-air staff want good ratings because when billings are down during low ratings, jobs may be eliminated.

Our major competitor usually had ratings in the mid to upper-

Falling for a Lie

teens. It was a great share of the market. They were quite a bit ahead of everyone else in the area. They had a monster promotional budget, did music and audience research on their own, and, generally, did everything right. If we didn't start off with a decent number for our first rating, we could be in trouble.

Thinking about her psychic abilities, I asked Maria, "What will our rating be?"

She closed her eyes. A moment later she tipped her head and raised an eyebrow. "I see a six or something."

Six? I wondered. *I surely wanted it to be higher than that! But . . . I suppose we could live with six for the first ratings period with the new format.*

The ratings company representative promised to call us late one afternoon to give us the preliminary numbers. They'd mail the complete report later. My air shift ran from three to seven, so the general manager said he'd take the call and then bring the results to me in the control room.

Three-thirty. Four o'clock. Four-thirty. Still no Len. I went to his office during a long record. His door was closed. I knocked. No answer. I knocked again. Nothing.

"Where's Len?" I asked the receptionist.

"He's gone for the day."

"Gone? He was supposed to tell me what the ratings were. Did they call?"

"Yes," she said, "and he left right after he took their call."

Puzzled, I headed back to the control room. During songs, I got the phone number of the ratings company and called them.

"Yes," said the female voice on other end of the line, "we did call your station with our report."

"Could you give it to me again, please? The manager must have forgotten and he left for the day."

"Let me get them." A moment later she spoke again. "Uh-h-h-h . . . did you change format during the ratings period?"

"No," I said. "We changed just before the ratings started. Why?"

"Well, I'm sorry, but you got a point six."

I grabbed pen and paper. "I missed that. A six point what?"

"No," she said. "POINT six."

Shock waves rumbled through me. "As in six-tenths of one percent?"

"You got it."

I passed the news on to the evening announcer when he came in. In the hallway a little later, I heard him say over the air, "I just got a request from our listener. Don't turn your dial, sir. Here's your song. Don't want to chance losing our entire audience!"

At home Maria took one look at me and asked, "What's wrong?"

I collapsed into a kitchen chair. "For years I've been working toward radio programming. Finally got the chance and I blew it."

"What do you mean?"

"My first and last chance," I moaned.

"Huh?"

"We got the preliminary ratings. You were right about the six, but I surely didn't understand where the decimal point would be."

"What was it?"

"Zero POINT six. As in six-tenths of one percent."

"So what'll happen?"

"Well . . . Len took the general manager job here right after the ratings period but before we received the results. I don't know him well enough to know how he'll react. But I could give you a pretty good picture of the norm for a general manager who just had their radio station ruined."

"Yeah?"

"They'd fire me on the spot."

Chapter Ten

"Will You Believe Us Now?"

Maria and I started talking about where we'd like to live and what kind of job I should look for. First thing the next morning, I went to see Len right away.

"Well," he said, "I want to look at the ratings when the full report comes before I decide what to do."

My execution was delayed.

"In the meantime," he added, "would you help do some research into what would be the best format for the listeners in Chattanooga. And let's get the others to help too."

I couldn't believe my ears. *He's asking me . . . the one who killed the station to help decide its future?* Frankly, I feared the "hole" for country music which I'd spotted earlier.

We researched and evaluated. Our main competitor had rock music tied up. It would be extremely expensive and difficult to unseat them. Our AM station played country music, but was being beaten pretty soundly by another AM station. There were no FM country music stations. We all agreed the one gaping need was FM country.

After we'd both had a chance to go over the full ratings report and our own research, Len asked me to join him in his office. "Shut the door behind you," he said.

My throat went dry. *Oh-oh! Here it comes!* Heart pounding, I closed the door and sat down.

"Well," he started, "we've done some pretty extensive research. What do you think? Should we continue with our rock format or change to country?"

In that instant all the thoughts of the last few weeks tumbled over each other in my mind. *If we stay with rock music, I might get to keep my job. If we change to country . . . well . . . the sum total of my country music knowledge is recognizing the names of Merle Haggard, Dolly Parton, and Willie Nelson. So, if we change to country, I get fired.*

I cleared my throat. "The big need here on FM is for a country music station. Chattanooga is ready for it. I think it could be a huge success."

I could already hear his response in my mind. *I agree. I'm sorry, but at this point I'm terminating your employment. . . .*

His voice broke through. "I agree." He turned away, cleared his throat, then faced me again. "Will you captain the ship?"

My mouth dropped open. *Huh? Me? I'm the one who just sank the station with the rock format!*

Then I heard myself saying, "Sure. I'll be glad to on two conditions."

Then reality hit. *Here I am . . . not being fired when by all rights I should be . . . and I'm giving my boss the conditions on which I'll accept his offer to save my job!*

"And the conditions are?" he asked.

Falling for a Lie

"First, that we don't fire any of the announcers. It's not their fault that the ratings were so bad. They all worked hard and are good people. They should be given the opportunity to choose to stay or leave."

"Agreed. Next?"

"That the format have a contemporary approach. I envision the station sounding exactly like it does now . . . very modern and with the same disc jockey approach . . . only we'd be playing country music instead."

"You've got a deal." He let that settle a few seconds then added, "I know you don't have experience with country. But I've watched you make decisions. You've got a good radio head. I have full confidence you can make it work."

So, now what? None of the staff knew country music. Should we pretend we did and try to fool the audience? Or should we admit we were beginners?

I chose the latter approach. It was honest. The listeners responded wonderfully. They'd call and tell us background information about the artists and other country trivia. Most of the staff became country music converts and the listeners loved it.

Then the next ratings period approached. We couldn't do much worse than we did last time. Any change would just about have to be for the better.

Moments of assurance alternated with misgivings the day the results should arrive. Midafternoon I heard Len let out a holler— "Fantastic!" He came tearing down the hall with a grin that looked like it might cut his head in half. He thrust the paper in front of me. "Look at this, Jay! I knew you could do it!"

I looked where he pointed. "WDOD - FM — 10."

"Ten? We made it from six tenths of one percent to ten percent in one ratings period?" I marveled.

"Will You Believe Us Now?"

"Yes, and look where we stand with the competition!"

WDOD - FM had shot to the Number One country music station slot in Chattanooga!

Within minutes the entire staff was whooping, hollering, and back-slapping. Thrilled with our accomplishments, we headed for greater heights.

Unfortunately, before long, Len accepted the general manager position at a station in Johnson City, Tennessee. I was stunned. He and I worked together well. I enjoyed working with him. From him I was learning a lot about management and about how to excel as a program director.

I missed Len's leadership. Often, when in a quandary at the station, I simply asked myself, "How would Len handle this?" Trying to think a thing through like Len did helped me keep success at the station.

Several months later I telephoned Len. "How are things going in Johnson City?"

"Well . . . I'm sure you've noticed in the ratings that the FM part of our station here in Johnson City is struggling. I've got to hire a new program director."

I applied for the job, then poured myself into it. During the last ratings period before I arrived, WQUT - FM claimed 10.6 percent of the market and was the number three station. Would my skills and work make a difference? Would we be able to take it to Number One?

Finally the ratings report for my first period arrived. WQUT - FM hadn't just jumped upward! It vaulted to 18.3 percent and the Number One slot. Success! I would keep working . . . at least for one more rating period!

The home ratings weren't necessarily the same. One evening Maria and I planned to go to a movie at seven o'clock—one that

Falling for a Lie

she especially wanted to see. I tried to do a few too many things, so we left a few minutes late. Maria was gracious about my error. We joked and laughed, looking forward to some much needed relaxation together. In line at the theater, the third person ahead of us got the last seat.

"How about 8:30?" the ticket clerk asked with a smile. "Same movie, same price."

I turned morose. "No thanks," I snapped, turning on my heels.

"Jay," Maria entreated as soon as she caught up with me, "Why don't we just go ahead and get tickets for 8:30 and go to dinner first rather than afterward?"

"Sorry I made us late," I snapped. "You wanted to see this movie and I made us late and . . ."

"It's no big deal," Maria insisted. "Let's just . . ."

The tone of my voice could have cut diamonds. "We planned this evening, and I messed it up."

"Eight-thirty is just as good for me as seven," she chirped.

My steps beat the sidewalk as Maria tried to keep up. "I ruined the evening," I snarled. At the car, I threw her door open, then slammed it behind her. I started the car.

"Honest, Jay, it doesn't matter," Maria pleaded. "We could still . . ."

I sighed deep, long, and loud, clearly communicating, "Shut up! And leave me alone!" I squealed the tires taking off.

Maria withdrew into silence. Halfway home, she exploded. "You didn't ruin anything till you started your pity party! I s'pose you're in one of your moods again. How long's this one going to last?"

Moods. Even at work, when I was in my you're-no-good-you'll-never-do-anything-right self-condemnation, everybody knew it and steered clear. My moods had been a source of friction with Susan and had a lot to do with a number of girlfriends deciding I was definitely not Prince Charming. I hated myself. I didn't hate anyone else. But how were they to know?

I'd just want to withdraw and think through the messes I got myself into and then get back to normal. But I'd left a wake of cutting words behind. The tone would have withered anything living. It was a lousy way to convince myself I could face life again, but I hadn't figured out another way.

I went to bed as soon as we got home. I don't know what Maria did.

One afternoon when I returned to the station after lunch, a cold wind drove biting rain. I shivered and pulled my coat tighter around me. When I entered, I heard pitiful wailing howls. "What's that?"

"A little dog," the receptionist said. "Found her outside—wet and freezing cold. I stuck her in the ladies' room so she could warm up and dry out."

I pushed the door open. A soaking wet black ball of fur a little bigger than a toy poodle raced out the door, down the hall, and into the lobby. She cowered under a chair in a corner, howling. I knelt and coaxed her. She inched toward me, her belly dragging the floor. When she got close to my fingers, she rolled over in submission. When I picked her up, her tiny body shook.

"Poor little thing's freezing," I said. I sat down across from the receptionist. "Let's write up an announcement. Found: Small black female dog, perhaps a toy poodle/terrier mix . . ."

The receptionist wrote while I comforted the trembling little creature. "Would you give the announcement to the deejay?" I asked. "In the meantime, I'll take her home to my wife. Dogs love her. She's even tamed raccoons, skunks, opossums, and rabbits. If anyone can calm a nervous animal, it's her."

At home, the little black dog snuggled into Maria's arms. The dog's trembling stopped almost immediately. Maria hadn't earned the title "Animal Lady" without reason.

After a few minutes, Maria suggested, "I'll go get her something to eat. Would you hold her?"

When I reached for the little dog, she shrank from me. When I grasped her, she started shaking again—not just a nervous quiver. Her whole body shook. She seemed scared to death.

Maria and I experimented and talked the situation over. Before long I telephoned the station: "Don't air the ad for the dog!" No way would I return her to a home where she must have been mistreated by a man. We'd keep her and love her.

Black as ink, the scared little creature soon became Inki, a happy, contented dog . . . as long as she could sit in Maria's lap or follow her like a shadow.

Even though Inki didn't trust me, I fell in love with her. Days turned to weeks. With much patience and gentleness on my part, Inki's shaking when I held her decreased to trembling. Eventually, to a tremor. After months of consistent kindness, Inki began to choose my lap rather than Maria's. That shocked us and anyone who knew Maria.

She and I still had our difficulties. Our personalities clashed. The fights got louder and longer. One evening during a calm between storms she asked, "How about if I leave for awhile?"

"Don't go. Let's work on it."

"But, supposedly, we *have* been working on it. If I leave temporarily, maybe we can be objective enough to see how to save our marriage."

We eventually agreed and she moved back to Wilmington. Inki stayed with me.

One evening at home, I turned on the TV and collapsed onto my bed. The sitcom bored me within minutes and I got up and switched channels. News. Another sitcom. For some reason I just kept turning the dial one more time.

As one picture flashed onto the screen, I felt like I'd been slapped across the face with a wet, ice-cold towel. My heart felt as if it stopped. I plunked backwards onto the edge of the bed. My eyes riveted onto the woman pushing the baby carriage.

It's her! . . . It can't be! . . . It is!

I scrunched down right in front of the television, examining the picture. *Her face is the same! . . . She moves the same! . . . She's wearing the same dress! . . . Her hair is the same! . . . It has to be her!*

My heart pounded as the PBS documentary continued. It showed actual file footage of the background story of the Charles Lindbergh, Jr. kidnapping. When it showed pictures of the Lindbergh estate—the house, the clearing, the surrounding woods—I felt very comfortable, almost as if I were going home after an absence.

But as the documentary continued, the shock of the first scene kept throbbing through my mind. *It's her! The nurse in this documentary is the woman I saw in vision four years ago. She is the woman I saw on the rooftop with two German-looking men and the child who ran and then fell off the building.*

"Is this enough?" the spirits seemed to ask. "How did you know when you watched the movie in Baltimore that Hauptman wasn't the right man? You couldn't have known if you hadn't been there. Why did you feel so comfortable in the setting of the Lindbergh home? Have we shown you enough? Will you believe us now?"

Chapter Eleven

Number One

How could I deny any longer that I was the reincarnation of the kidnapped Lindbergh baby?

But I didn't want to be. I didn't want to be anyone from a former life who would draw attention to me now. I just wanted to accomplish what I was here in a physical body to learn. I wanted to work off my negative karma as quickly as possible and move on to higher spiritual planes in as short a time as possible.

I'd puzzled over my Lindbergh curiosity for years. Knowing was worse than wondering.

Others had claimed to be Charles Lindbergh, Jr. Some alleged they'd been kidnapped and adopted and were now, in the same life, the grown Lindbergh son. Some said they were a reincarnation of the Lindbergh baby. Because of my fascination with the Lindberghs and my belief in reincarnation, I'd researched the claims of numerous Charles Lindbergh, Jr. would-be's. I knew the ridicule they experienced. I wanted no part of it.

What difference did it make anyway? Why had the spirits teased me since I was a toddler? Why had they harassed me with questions? "So what am I to do, God?"

Silence.

My mind went back to early days when I paid attention to Bible stories. I pictured Jesus and the disciples in a little boat with a wild storm whipping the Sea of Galilee over them. The storm was so ferocious that even experienced fishermen panicked. But when all seemed lost, as another flash of lightning tore across the sky, one of the disciples caught a glimpse of Jesus . . . sleeping. The desperate fisherman shook his Master. "We're about to die! Wake up!" Jesus stood up, stretched out His arms, and said, "Peace." Waves dropped where they were. In minutes, the water was glassy.

"God," I prayed, "Jesus brought peace to water and wind when He lived down here. Couldn't You bring peace to me?" I heard no answer. Frustration settled over me.

A telephone call from Maria brought hope. We agreed that Jodi, who was staying with me for the summer, and I would meet Maria in Virginia at a spot I'd wanted for years to visit—the center Edgar Cayce had established to further his work.

Hugh Lynn had died, but Gladys Davis, the person who had transcribed all of Edgar Cayce's readings and speeches while he was living, still worked at the center. Eager for Maria and Jodi to meet her, I spoke to her secretary. "Good morning. I'm Jay Christian. I visited with Hugh Lynn and met Gladys when they came to Selma to dedicate the plaque marking Edgar Cayce's photography studio. Is there any chance my wife and daughter could just briefly greet her?"

"I'm sorry," she said, kindly but definitely. "She's booked with half-hour appointments two to three months ahead most of the time. There's no way I can get you in to see her today."

Falling for a Lie

"I understand that. I'm not talking about sitting down to talk with her. But between appointments, would it be possible for her just to meet my wife and daughter? Just to shake hands and say 'Hello'?

She raised an eyebrow ever so slightly. "Have a seat. I'll check with her. What was your name?"

"Jay Christian." I handed her a business card.

We waited briefly. The secretary returned. "Follow me, please."

She led us down a hall, to a conference room. "Gladys will be in shortly."

Before long, Gladys Davis walked through the door then closed it. She smiled and held out her hand to me. "Good morning, Jay. How are you?"

She greeted Maria and Jodi warmly, then sat down at the table with us. Relaxed, she reminisced about Edgar and Hugh Lynn Cayce and answered our questions. For half an hour, she acted as though nothing in the world was more important to her than us.

That visit increased my love and respect for the Cayces and their ministry. It strengthened the bond I had felt with both Edgar and Hugh Lynn. It raised my spirits for a while.

And we decided Maria would come back shortly. I'd try to be less moody. We'd both try to communicate calmly rather than blowing up. Could we make it?

But, even with Maria home, I still felt restless. I was puzzled by the long silence from the spirits, the lack of direction. I tried to ignore the emptiness I felt. If I steered the station to success and kept control in the process, maybe I'd sense fulfillment.

One morning I prepared for a ten o'clock appointment at the station with a rating company representative. Ten, then 10:30, came and went. I was miffed that she didn't bother to call and let me know she'd be late. Eleven, 11:30. By then, concerned for her safety, I telephoned her company.

"She what?" Ire poured through my voice after her manager told me she had gone that morning, instead, to our station's biggest local rival.

Irritation simmered. By the time she arrived at 1:30, my lid was about to blow. I ushered her curtly to a place at the long glass table in our conference room. Our executive assistant joined us to take notes.

I turned to the rating company rep. "By the way," I asked coolly, "didn't we have appointment at ten o'clock this morning?"

She swallowed. "Yes, we did. And . . ."

"Here it is 1:30 in the afternoon!" I stormed, tipping my chair back. "I didn't even know you were going to meet with our competitors at all. Why didn't you tell us?"

Stone-faced, she started to open her mouth.

Before she could speak, I railed on. "A couple hours ago, I was concerned for your safety! I had to call your company to find out where you were. We have plenty to do around here other than twiddle our thumbs waiting. I find your attitude to be very unprofessional and . . ."

A sharp *cra-a-ack* resounded through the room as the back of my chair snapped. I fell backward, my feet jerking into the air. I did a complete backflip, landing face down on the carpet, all six-feet-five-inches of me sprawled across the floor.

I pulled myself onto hands and knees and crawled back to the table. Stiff old me—I couldn't loosen up for anything. Still on my knees, I planted my elbow on the table and shook my finger at the rep. "And furthermore . . ."

The representative's only reaction was a slight . . . ever so slight . . . upturn at the corners of her mouth.

One afternoon a few weeks later, while I was working in my

office, Len stepped in, closed the door, and sat down. "I have an idea."

"Great." I respected Len's knowledge and management skills. His ideas were always worth listening to. "Let's hear it."

"You have good ideas, Jay. You have a great sense for what makes radio work. There's no doubt in my mind you're going to go places in programming. But I'm wondering if one little thing might make you even more effective."

"What's that?"

"What would happen if you'd spend a little more time with your crew?"

I already told the employees what I expected of them. I told them about changes. I evaluated air checks with them. "Like . . . what do you mean?" I asked.

"It's obvious to me, Jay, that you like the staff members. And you work to keep life good for them. But I don't think *they* know you appreciate them."

"They don't?"

"No. I don't think so." He shifted in his chair. "You tend to be all business. You have a job to do and you're going to accomplish it no matter what it takes. Right?"

I nodded. "Yeah. You have me pegged."

"I appreciate your working hard," Len continued. "That's how you took this station to 18.3 percent of the market and Number eighteen in the nation. But you really need to pull yourself away from your desk at least a couple times a day. Go talk with the office staff, the announcers, the sales staff. Relax. Be personable. They'll work with you better if they know you as a person and if they know you care about them."

I loved the challenge of programming and accomplished a massive amount of work. *But small talk?* My stomach did somersaults just thinking about it. Frankly, I wasn't interested in my co-workers getting to know me. I had problems enough without that. Maybe I could ask all the questions—get to know them without them getting to know me. Whatever, the management books I'd read agreed with Len. If it was the right thing to do, I'd do it.

"You're probably right," I admitted. "I'll try."

Pulling myself away from work to be personable was harder work than work. And ultimately more fearsome!

Weeks slipped into months. It did seem like cooperation improved. Ratings inched upward too—19.2 percent of the market and Number 8 in the nation.

Work was going well. After I'd been in Johnson City a few months, Len asked if I'd consider doing the operations manager job for both the AM and FM stations along with continuing to program the FM. *Well . . . it would be a promotion . . . and I've always liked challenges!*

Heart and soul went into that job—mine and those of the entire staff. The arrival of ratings reports became exciting events. The ratings climbed till WQUT - FM was the highest-rated radio station, by quarter hour, in the country. Not just in Johnson City, but the *whole* country! In comparison with every other radio station in the United States!

Then my own afternoon show hit Number One in the country!

The station as a whole was succeeding. I was succeeding. I'd only been prouder when Jodi was born!

Jockeying for top billing was constant. But when we slipped out of Number One position, we were usually somewhere in the top ten of all stations of various formats and in the top five of all rock stations in the country. And, when my show missed the top spot, it was in the top five most of the time. Work was wonderful!

Falling for a Lie

Then there was home. My dedication to radio and the hours and energy I poured into professional success didn't leave much for nurturing marriage. We both tried, but we just couldn't squelch the fireworks.

Should we divorce? If it wasn't the right thing to do, we'd only have to work off negative karma in another life. Still friends, we ended the marriage.

With Maria gone, I poured myself all the more into work. The station's ratings stayed at the top. *Radio & Records,* the premiere trade magazine in the business, printed several articles about my success. Of course, it felt good. And their ratings reports continued to list me and the station in the top spots.

So why the empty feeling when I stop long enough to think?

Chapter Twelve

It's in the Numbers

So why the empty feeling? I haven't had a vision in several years. Haven't heard from the spirits since right after the documentary.

I immersed myself in more books about reincarnation, including several books by Ruth Montgomery, a spiritualist who would sit at a typewriter and give herself over to the spirits. She'd type a question, then just sit there with her fingers poised over the typewriter keys. She believed that the messages her fingers typed in response to the questions came from a group of spirits whose purpose was to enlighten the world on the reality of life after death, reincarnation, and the path to God.

One day in the newspaper I read an article about a group of mostly Baby Boomers who described their philosophy as "New Age." I'd never heard the term, but the further I read, the more excited I got. They believed the same things I did! I knew very few people who shared my ideas. But according to this, there were thousands all over the country. The title in itself was a relief—I'd no longer

Falling for a Lie

have to use the term "occult" to describe my beliefs.

My radio success in Johnson City caught other station managers' attention. From time to time I received job offers. For nearly four years I had turned them all down. I loved Johnson City, and my work, and the staff.

In radio, cities are ranked by population into "markets." Usually, the larger the market where you work, the more money you make, and the more successful you are considered. Johnson City was about the eighty-fifth market. Every time I turned down an offer in a larger area, a question nagged at me: *Could I make it in the big time?*

Eventually the question wore me down. I had to find out. *No matter how happy I am in my work here,* I told myself, *if I don't give a larger market a try, the opportunity may pass.* I was willing to accept failure as the possible price for finding out.

WGKX - FM in Memphis, known as KIX 106, made me an offer. It was in about the fifty-third size radio market, a nice move up. And it played Country. As much as I'd enjoyed Johnson City, I had missed country music.

The offer wasn't perfect. The manager's first choice for program director had accepted the position then bowed out a couple days later. The manager made it clear from the beginning that I was second choice. *But I've gained others' full confidence after working with them a while,* I reasoned. *Surely I can overcome the resistance here too.*

Inki and I moved to Memphis. Eager to prove I could be successful in a larger market, I immersed myself in making plans and carrying them out.

One off-work afternoon, I meandered through a boat show. I'd intended only to relax a couple hours. Instead I left with an appointment to check out a partially-built, custom-made, seventeen foot runabout/ski boat with inboard/outboard motor.

I loved water and small boats. And I could make one more payment a month. The salesman edged me over a few objections. I left with a signed agreement to purchase the boat when it was completed in a month. Besides, Keyli, my current romantic interest, would enjoy it too.

I had met Keyli at a remote broadcast in Johnson City after Maria had left. Between her alluring almond eyes and her southern accent, I didn't catch her name at first. "Keyli," she repeated. "'Key,' like a car key, and 'lee,' as in Robert E. Lee. Keyli."

Life had its ups and downs in Memphis, but through them all I kept in contact with Keyli. I told her about my beliefs in reincarnation and she joined me in the New Age thinking. The strong bond we felt from the beginning of our friendship convinced us we must have been together in previous lifetimes. It seemed destiny had brought us together now.

But I was cautious. It seemed like everyone who got to know me very well rejected me. In both work and personal relationships, I'd been through way too many cycles: first, attraction; then a honeymoon season where all went well; when people got to know me, we became disillusioned with each other; then we'd separate—I'd go on to another job or another girlfriend or wife thinking maybe this would be the situation that would bring me happiness.

At Johnson City, though, I'd proved I could do better. My efforts to be personable paid off. Rather than turning sour, my working relationships got better and better. The staff actually wanted me to stay—not just management, everyone. They even gave me a going away party. Had I conquered the ugly cycle at work? Would my success carry over into a romantic relationship? I couldn't stand another rejection.

There was no question I was Number One in Keyli's mind.

Falling for a Lie

Her admiring eyes and assurances convinced me we could face forever together.

Unfortunately, overcoming the resistance of this manager was a larger-than-life challenge. Our management styles did not mesh well. And perhaps I was too direct about my concerns.

A month before Keyli and I planned to marry, the radio station handed me a real wallop—a pink slip.

Even though our management styles clashed, the manager liked me, thought I was a good announcer, and offered me a job announcing.

"I really appreciate your offer," I told him, "but I plan to move in the direction of programming and management, rather than announcing."

"Why don't you stay for a month, anyway, while you look for a new job. We'll keep you on the payroll. You can use the station phone for contacts."

I could hardly believe my ears. When most stations fired an employee, they ran them off the property and didn't give another thought about their well-being. I accepted his generous offer.

That evening I told Keyli. "I've got some good news and some bad news. The good news is . . . I won't have any trouble getting off time for a honeymoon."

"Wonderful!" she exulted.

"Don't be too quick," I cautioned. "The bad news is . . ."

"Yes?"

"I'm looking for a job."

"What?"

"I got fired today."

We discussed things a bit before I suggested, "Keyli, radio is a very unstable profession. If you marry me, you'll likely have to face this sort of thing again someday. And no one knows how often!

You might have to leave a city you love."

"I don't care," she said. "I love you."

"Just because I was the Number One disc jockey in the nation when you met me doesn't mean life will always go that well. Maybe you ought to reconsider. I'll understand if you want to back out. Life with me could . . ."

"No!" she interrupted. "I don't want to back out! I don't care how many jobs you lose! I don't care how many times we have to move! Losing a job is much too small a thing to interfere with my love for you!"

So we married as planned, honeymooned in Mexico, and came back to Memphis. I continued looking for work from KIX 106.

Sure losing a job was a downer, but anyone could get fired sometime in their working years. No sense letting it get me down. My reputation was good. And well-known.

Before long, I had a choice. Though I'm not at all fond of cold weather, the position of operations manager at WGAR - AM/FM in Cleveland, Ohio was more temptation than I could refuse. Cleveland was only a few hours' drive from Jodi. The job was in management. The expectations seemed reasonable. And Cleveland was about the twentieth largest market in the country. A good move up!

By the time I arrived, the company had already hired three broadcasting consultants to evaluate the market potential. I looked over their predictions then did my own market research. I devised a format to meet the unique tastes of our target audience in Cleveland. After some calculating of my own, I felt we could do better than any of the consultants' predictions and set about to make it happen. Only time would tell. I wavered between eager and anxious for our first ratings.

Jodi graduated from high school while I lived in Cleveland. As

Falling for a Lie

I sat in the football stadium watching her march by in cap and gown, I remembered the day she was born and all the hope I had then of being a good father. I relived her departure when she was only eighteen months old. I remembered the summer vacations she stayed with me and the myriad motel visits when I drove to see her. I relived spending every Christmas with her.

Yes, I'd missed out on some great job opportunities because I wouldn't move more than a day's drive away from Jodi. That didn't matter. There wasn't one sacrifice that wasn't worth the trouble. Susan had been fair with me and had raised Jodi well. And I'd helped all I could. Pride swelled in me as I thought about the beautiful young lady Jodi had grown to be—both inside and out.

One day at the station, our morning announcer interviewed a numerologist on air. Nancy touted the benefits of determining fortune and fate through a system of exchanging numbers for letters, adding them up, and determining the positive or negative value. According to numerology, you could also take someone's name and determine their personality, to a degree.

Unhappy with yourself? Change your name to fit a number for a personality you like, and *voila!* New person. How about that house you want to buy? Add up the street address, use the formula to change names into numbers, and, if it's a positive number, the house is for you. If not, avoid it! Looking for a spouse? Use the formula on the name of someone who interests you. If it's a compatible number with yours, proceed. If not, keep looking.

Nancy's theories and testimonies fascinated me. I made a point to meet her before she left the station. It didn't take her long to sense my interest. She invited me to bring my wife to her home for more information.

Keyli and I visited Nancy a few evenings later. Over the ensuing months, we became good friends, discussing numerology, reincarnation, astrology, spiritualism, and more. We also attended some of the meetings she held in her home featuring local, everyday people who had developed some skill as mediums or numerologists. Nancy was a wonderful person with a warm and enthusiastic personality.

Numerology became a big part of our lives. Many times we pored over charts on Nancy's kitchen table, planning our work and personal lives. She also became a popular radio guest on our morning show, doing numerology readings for listeners.

Everything seemed to be going well at the station. Then it was finally time to get the ratings report.

The very first rating period I was there our AM/FM signals beat the consultants' projected highest possible figures, moving into third place in the city. Our morning announcer was rated second, as well.

I was jubilant! I could be successful in larger markets!

The staff worked hard and had a great time. Our ratings continued to inch upward. We got a lot of attention from Cleveland listeners and the local press. Even the national radio trade magazines were writing stories about our success. We had gone far beyond the ratings the station had ever attained or hoped to attain as a country station, and we were within challenging distance of its former glory ratings when it was a powerhouse pop station. All went well until the manager left.

The new general manager's experience was in sales, not programming; in rock music, not country. And his management style was far different than mine. Not wrong, necessarily. But very, very different. Right away, I started looking for another job.

But I like Cleveland, I pondered one day. *So does my wife. Why let Darrel run me off. If I stay, perhaps I can move up in the chain of stations this company owns.*

Besides, I liked challenges. I had a track record of remarkable

Falling for a Lie

success at this station. I'd had numerous compliments from the home office, from people whom I highly respected. Since I was doing a better job than anyone else had, even beating the best projections for the station, I figured that management would recognize my value to the company. Surely we could find a way to settle our differences.

So I quit looking elsewhere and fought hard for the programming I believed would keep the ratings soaring. Did I fight too hard?

Chapter Thirteen

From the Jaws of Success

At six one evening, Darrel called me into his office. "I haven't been happy with your performance, Jay. I've hired someone to take your place." He turned, picked up a box from beside his chair, and offered it to me. "Here's a box for the personal effects from your desk. You need to clean it out . . . now."

He followed me to my office and stood guard as if to keep me from carrying off the desk. When I finished, he escorted me out. We stepped through the front door. He held out his hand, open palm up. "The key?"

"Oh yeah." The firing had happened so quickly I hadn't even thought about the key. I sat the box down on the walk, pulled my keys from my pocket, twisted the station key off the ring, and handed it to him.

He snapped his fingers closed around the key, whirled, yanked the door open, and strode down the hall.

I trudged to my car, hardly believing the last few minutes. *Sure.*

Falling for a Lie

It was obvious Darrel and I didn't see eye to eye. But getting fired? After I turned the station around and brought them success they didn't dream possible?

Defeat. Defeat spit from the jaws of success.

At home, I hugged Keyli. "I'm not really a prophet, but . . ."

She tipped her head up, her dark eyes searching mine. "Huh?"

"Remember my saying that radio is an unstable profession?"

"Yeah."

"I knew it was always possible I could get fired again someday. I didn't think it would be from the next job."

Keyli's left eyebrow jutted up. "Are you saying . . .?" Letting her half-question hang, she searched my eyes.

"I'm saying, I just got fired."

"How could they?"

"Pretty easily, I guess."

"But look what you did for them! Doesn't that mean anything?"

"That's what makes it so frustrating. Before Darrel arrived, I was the golden boy of the company. The president of the national chain that owns this station bragged to others about my performance. And last time he was here he was full of praise. 'Jay, we're so proud of what you're doing. We're thrilled with the success of the station. It's obvious you're the stimulus behind it. We're thrilled to have you with our company.' "

"So where is he now?" Keyli asked.

"Nowhere to be seen—right alongside the other corporate officers that praised me up one side and down the other a few months ago."

"So, what did he use for a reason to fire you?"

"Reason? Who needs a reason?" I sneered. "He gave some excuses. Like, I didn't follow all the recommendations the chain program director gave. That's so phony! I specifically asked Darrel, 'Am I to treat his recommendations as suggestions or directives? Am I supposed to implement them no matter what I think? Or do I still have the choice to use what I think is valuable and not use what I don't think is right for our station?' Of course I did tell him I wasn't responsible for any downturns in the ratings if I wasn't actually making the programming decisions."

"And what did he say?"

"He assured me I was still in charge of programming and I could make the choice. And every one of the recommendations were over very minor things. After the written recommendations arrived, I asked again, 'Do I have to implement these changes or do I have the choice what to use and what not to use?' He still assured me it was my choice. So I used some and didn't use what seemed inappropriate for our station and our goals. It surely seems, though, that the fact that I made a choice was a major part of his excuse for firing me."

I slumped into my chair at the table. "The only 'reason' he had was my anger. I did lose my temper twice. Maybe three times."

Both Keyli and I picked at dinner.

"Can you find a job here?" Keyli asked.

"I don't know."

"I only have a couple months left in nursing school."

"Whatever happens, you can finish school. But what if I can get a lot better job some other place?"

"I really don't want to move."

"I didn't want to get fired either."

The next morning I started calling radio contacts. Even though I'd just been fired, my reputation was known. Since my daughter was an adult now, I didn't limit my search to within driving distance of her home.

Falling for a Lie

Between calls, I evaluated my contribution to the dis-ease at the last jobs. Two firings in a row was more than enough.

One evening I heard from a disc jockey who had worked for me in another area. I'd fired him then relented after he begged and pleaded for an hour, assuring me he'd live by stringent guidelines. He met his end of the bargain. More than a year later, he left our station and I hadn't heard from him since.

But after I was fired, he called, "Heard you were fired, Jay. I just wanted to encourage you. You're good at what you do. You'll find another job."

"So how's it going for you?" I asked.

"Well," he said. "You may be interested to know, I got a chance to go into programming. I grabbed it. Finally, a chance to run radio the way I knew it should be run!

"Just one problem," he continued. "Our station's ratings took a nose-dive. And nothing I did helped. One day I said to myself, 'My way's not working. Who's succeeding in programming?' Immediately I thought of you. You did wonders in Johnson City. And repeated them in Cleveland. So, whenever I had to make a decision, I started asking myself, 'What would Jay do?'

"You know, Jay, for being so stupid when you were my supervisor and I had all the answers, you sure got smart. As soon as I started doing things the way I thought you would, the ratings turned around and headed up again. I'm doing really well. And I've got you to thank. With the record you've got, Jay, you're not going to have any trouble finding another job."

His call encouraged me.

Shortly, out of Cleveland's ashes rose San Francisco. At KNEW, part of an AM/FM combination, the AM station was suffering big losses—had been going downhill fast for a year. Usually when AM listeners abandon a station and go to FM, it's extremely hard to get them back. Besides, there were more than eighty radio stations in the San Francisco area. They were looking for a new program director who would also be the afternoon drive announcer. My interest in the job centered around expectations. Were they realistic?

From the interview, all looked bright. My own figuring assured me their goals were reasonable. Was this finally the job where I could use my skills and be appreciated?

After the last fiasco, I wanted to give myself every advantage—I used numerology to check the name San Francisco, the call letters of the station, the names of people at the station I'd be working with, apartment addresses. Everything checked out fine except my name. But with changing Jay to just the letter J, the number went from negative to positive. So I changed my radio name from Jay Christian to J. Christian. Everything was set for success!

It was exciting to be in a big company in the fourth-largest radio market in the country. My first goal was to stop the ratings from going down. If we could just slow the descent for the first ratings period, I'd be happy. If we were flat—going neither up or down—I'd be thrilled. That would mean the decline was over and we were starting back up.

I researched market and music. I chose new music, coached a crew of top-notch announcers, devised contests, and took care of a host of details besides filling the afternoon announcer position.

Keyli finished school in Cleveland then joined Inki and me in the San Francisco area. It didn't take her long to feel at home there.

Life had never looked brighter on all fronts. Though I received only rare visions, I checked decisions with numerology. Wasn't that an assurance of knowing the right decisions to prepare for tomorrow? Wasn't it practically a guarantee for success?

At home, Keyli and I continued to get along well. We discussed decisions sanely—no yelling or temper tantrums. In our

Falling for a Lie

entire dating and marriage relationship we had never even argued. I had overcome the nasty moods that had soured past relationships— Keyli had never had to endure them. *Finally*, I thought occasionally, *I've broken the negative cycles that ruined my life before.* Keyli's sparkling, almond eyes, her warm smile, her charm assured me over and over that I was Number One to her no matter what the world around me thought. Life was good!

"Don't you ever get any ideas about leaving me," Keyli crooned, smiling up into my eyes, " 'cause I'm gonna love you the rest of your life and I'll never in a dozen lifetimes let you go without the biggest fight any divorce court ever dreamed of."

She'd said this on occasion before. I always responded the same: "I hope you always want to stay. But if you ever change your mind, I'll be the easiest guy in the world to get rid of. I love you enough to want *you* to be happy."

Keyli found a job she loved, and I felt the same about mine. After twenty years of aiming high and working hard, of discouraging failures and heartening successes, I'd made it to the big time. Probably less than five percent of those who work in radio ever made it to a position of this prestige in a market the size of the San Francisco area. I was well paid to do a job I loved in the specific place where I wanted to live. And I was getting along with the staff.

One question remained. I'd made it to the big time. Could I succeed here? We wouldn't know about that until ratings.

At the staff Christmas party, the general manager took me aside and said, "We're real happy with your performance, J. We hope you're with us for a long time." Shortly, the preliminary ratings were released. The general manager, operations manager, and I stood at the fax machine watching every line as it printed. First came the 12+ rating. We were down. But then the 25 to 54 ratings line printed. I couldn't believe my eyes. I stared at it.

"Do you see that?" I exploded. "Our target audience! Up two tenths of a point!"

"Great!" one of them said.

I couldn't contain my delight. "Up. From 1.2 to 1.4. In the first quarter! We didn't just slow or stop the decline! We did both *and* started back up!"

In the next few days, all of us congratulated the announcers and other staff and rejoiced over our success.

Karma was finally smiling on me!

Weeks later when I quit spinning records at 7:00 p.m. I noticed that Ron, the operations manager, was still in his office. *Why's he still here tonight?* I wondered.

As I approached my office, he stepped into the hall. "Can we talk?"

Ron was usually friendly, jovial. Now his voice sounded strained. My shoulders tensed. "Sure," I said, trying to sound casual.

He motioned me to a chair. "Uh-h-h," he stuttered, staring first at my left shoulder, then at the floor.

Why won't he look me in the eye? I wondered.

Ron slouched into the chair behind his desk. Our eyes met. Silence hung like a bomb waiting to explode. Finally I forced words between dry lips. "What's happening?"

He looked down at his cluttered desktop and came right to the point. "The company's decided to make some changes. Unfortunately, you're one of them. As of now, you're done as program director."

Chapter Fourteen

The Crash

Sitting there in my boss's office, I felt like a heavyweight boxing champion had just slammed his fist into the side of my head. Still reeling, I heard Ron speak again.

"We didn't sign a contract when you came to work here . . ."

I gasped. Then breathed in deeply and exhaled slowly, trying to relax enough to grasp what was happening.

"but if we had, we would have signed you on for a year. We'll honor that. . . ."

I sighed.

"There are a couple options. You can stay on as a full-time disc jockey for the next six months, but then the job's over. Of course, your wages will drop. OR you can go now and we'll give you a cash settlement to help tide you over till you get another job."

I couldn't believe what I was hearing. "Why?"

"Well, you know, the ratings haven't been as good as we'd like."

"What do you mean?" I countered. His expression didn't

change. I pressed on. "When I accepted this programming position, the ratings were sliding downhill fast—clear down to 1.2. The goals we agreed on for my first full year were to bring the ratings up to 2.0 in the target 25 to 54 age group. In three months, I stopped the downward spiral. I'd have been happy this first rating period if it had held even. But I haven't just stopped the ratings from going lower they've already turned around and started up!"

"But in the 12-plus . . ."

"Sure, the 12-plus went down. You know as well as I do that you can't attract thirteen-year-olds and fifty-year-olds with the same programming. You told me not to worry about all the others, that 25 to 54 was our focus group, to turn around the ratings in the 25 to 54 age group at all cost."

"But in the 55 and up . . ."

"Fifty-five and up wasn't who you asked me to attract." *Why wouldn't he listen?* "I did exactly what we agreed on. And I did it faster than anyone thought possible."

Ron squirmed.

I finally broke cold silence. "I am *really* surprised!"

"I am too." Ron sighed. He seemed like a puppet moving on invisible strings, like a man forced by some superior to carry out an action with which he disagreed. He shifted in his chair and cleared his throat. "But, we'd better get back to the options."

Both Keyli and I had grown to love the San Francisco Bay area. "So, if I deejay the next six months, any chance I can continue?" I asked. "Or is it absolutely, written-in-concrete that on my anniversary date I'm gone?"

"You're gone," he said.

"Can I tell you in the morning?"

"Morning's fine."

In my office, I plopped into my chair and swiveled toward the

Falling for a Lie

window. One of the benefits of the job of program director at this station had been the view out the office window—a marina, the Estuary, and Alameda Island. From this Jack London Square office in Oakland, any time of day or night I could look out and watch speedboats, freighters, military ships. During high-pressure days the sailboats, cabin cruisers, and yachts had been my tranquilizer.

Yesterday I was at the pinnacle of success. Suddenly it hit me: *Fired. From the third job in a row.*

I didn't like getting fired the other times either. But they were no surprise. I understood why. I'd had disagreements and personality conflicts with management. But I'd dealt with those issues. Everything had seemed good here. So, why did I get fired? I didn't have a clue of any valid reason.

I turned from the window. Whether I stayed or not, I'd no longer have the office. I numbly cleared my personal belongings from the desk—pens, a letter opener, a list of business contacts. I lifted my wife's and daughter's photographs from the wall. One last look then I was gone.

Why? my mind screamed as I plodded down the stairs. I trudged down the sidewalk along the Estuary toward my Jeep Cherokee. Ripples nudging against the pier taunted me, "You're just not good enough! You'll never deserve success." Desperation swirled the words round and round like a cracked record.

City streets, the Caldecott Tunnel, freeway miles, more streets to my apartment in Pleasant Hill. I know I drove it, but it was a blur of cars zooming past me—like everyone in real life was passing me up. Of sirens screaming, "Failure! J. Christian, you're a failure!" Of street lights blinking, "Caution—you obviously don't know how to make it. Stop—get off the spiral downward."

"My job's done," I told my wife, Keyli. "We've got two choices. I can deejay six months with a smaller salary then leave, or I can leave now with severance pay."

Inki bounced into my lap and nuzzled my hand. She always seemed to sense when something was wrong.

As our discussion continued, Keyli liberally tossed in her evaluation of the decision-makers at the station: "They're nuts!" "They don't know what they're doing!" "You turned that station around—it's gaining an audience again. What do they think they're doing?"

My wife was with me. At least this marriage was solid. Keyli doted on me. I sensed I'd depend a lot on her assurances in the coming weeks.

Next morning I told Ron, "I'll take the money." He seemed surprised. The bookkeeper cut me a check and I was gone.

Yesterday I was program director for a major station in a big-time radio market. Today I was unemployed. Yesterday I was earning good money, well able to pay high rent, payments on two new vehicles and a boat, and minimum payments on our maxed-out credit cards. Today I didn't know when or from where the next dollar was coming. Yesterday writers wrote success stories about me in national radio trade journals. Today a bookkeeper wrote my final check. Yesterday I was a success. Today I was a failure.

I'd willingly given my profession everything—way more hours than were required, all the physical and mental energy I could muster. I'd turned struggling stations around. In spite of success, I'd gotten fired from the last three stations.

Why is this happening to me? I wondered. *What am I doing wrong?* I had followed the numerologist's advice precisely. *I've done everything I know to do. And I'm still failing. What will tomorrow bring?*

Discouraged beyond anything I'd experienced before, I craved Keyli's support and friendship. She was the last prop that held up my sanity.

She comforted me, encouraged me, assured me. "You helped put me through L.P.N. school," she said at breakfast one morning. "I'm working now and enjoying my job. Why don't you go back to school? I'll support us while you train for something you'd really like to do."

"Me?" I questioned, surprised at the thought. "What would I take?"

"What would you really like to do?"

We crunched toast and talked about every career either of us could think of. "Know what I'd really like to do?" I finally concluded.

"What?"

"Radio."

She looked, dumbfounded, across the table at me and blinked slowly. "But . . ."

"I love radio. I'm good at it. I can't think of anything I'd rather do."

A few days later, I felt a coolness slipping into Keyli's affections. Nothing I could put my finger on. Just a sense that something wasn't as it used to be. *Forget it,* I told myself, *I'm probably just paranoid now.*

Then Keyli gave me a Valentine card covered with hearts and roses—the biggest, prettiest card she'd *ever* given me . . . and she'd added a handwritten, mushy note. I quit worrying and threw myself harder into job-hunting.

Unemployment stretched into weeks. At home, Keyli's activities contradicted her card. She slept later than usual and left earlier than necessary for work. In between, I tried to talk with her.

"I interviewed at a radio station in Marin today. If I get the job, we could move to an apartment between your job and mine and stay in the area. What do you think?"

She responded blandly. "We can talk about it if you get it."

Sometimes I asked, "What's wrong, Keyli?"

"Nothing."

Or, "Keyli, what am I doing that frustrates you?"

"Let's not talk about it now."

Keyli had locked me out of her life. No matter how hard I searched, I couldn't find the key. A month after I was fired, I joined her one evening in the hospital cafeteria during her supper break. We chatted a bit. But she squirmed and avoided looking me in the eye even when we talked about the rain. Finally I asked again, "What's wrong, Keyli?"

"Oh, nothing."

"You've said that before," I countered, "but *something's* wrong." I reached over and touched her arm gently. "Do you want to work on it, or do you want us to go our separate ways?"

The question just fell out of my mouth. But I figured it was OK. I wanted to get to the bottom of this, to identify the problem, and fix it. The obvious answer was "To work on it." I was willing to do whatever it took to resurrect Keyli's warm smile, to make her dark eyes dance again. Not only did I love her, she and Inki were all I had left. I desperately needed to hear Keyli say she valued our relationship.

Keyli swallowed her bite of sandwich. Our eyes met for an instant. She dropped her glance back to her plate and whispered, "To go our separate ways."

Chapter Fifteen

"Can You Tell Me Why?"

To go our separate ways? I couldn't believe my ears. I searched Keyli's face for an inkling of hope. Her eyes were ice.

For two more weeks I tried everything I could think of to get Keyli to talk, to get her to tell me why she was unhappy, what I could do. "Let's go to a marriage counselor," I urged.

"The decision's made," she snapped. "Besides, Marta told me karma was obviously at work between us. You must have divorced me in a previous life. Now fate's paying you back."

So that was it. A friend at work had convinced her to leave me. "But . . . what if this is our *first* divorce?" I pleaded.

A blank look crossed her face.

"If we go through with this," I continued, "we'll probably end up marrying again in a future life. And again and again until it works."

Keyli stood there, stone still. *Is there hope?* I dared to question. *If we can just talk, we can solve anything.*

"Forget it," she snapped, breaking the long silence. "There's no more to talk about!" She stomped out.

If I could just figure out what was going on I'd be OK. If only I could find a reason. I might not like it, but I could deal with it. But I couldn't squeeze a sound reason for my getting fired out of my boss. And, clearly, Keyli doesn't plan to give any further explanations for wanting a divorce.

The next morning I didn't bother to dress, take a shower, shave, or comb my hair. Nor the following day. Just mostly laid in bed wondering. Neither Keyli nor I opened the drapes. Shortly I lost track of what day it was or even whether it was day or night.

Wish I had a gun. Just the thought would have shocked me before. I'd never been able to comprehend how anyone could consider suicide, let alone do it. Now the idea seemed inviting.

Hours plodded on. Once in a while I turned on the television. The talk show about numerology would have fascinated me a few days before. I switched it off. *What would I want with numerology? So much for its guarantees of success! If I ever do work in radio again, I'll change my name back to Jay.*

I toyed with the idea of suicide. The more I thought about it, the better it sounded. *But what would happen to Inki?* I wondered.

Inki, obviously, had made no plans to leave me. Not for a day. Not for a second. Constantly, she lay on my stomach or snuggled close beside me. On the rare occasion that I wandered to the bathroom or kitchen, she tripped along beside me.

I lay in bed day after day, feeling numb. Yet pain beyond belief clawed at me constantly.

Shortly after I was fired, I'd made reservations to go to Nashville's annual Country Radio Seminar, hoping to network and find job leads. Now, I had to force myself out of bed to pack a suitcase.

At the seminar, the various record companies hosted entertainment suites to attract attendees to their advertising. In addition to celebrities, drinks, and munchies, one record company provided a psychic.

Would she have some answers for me? Might she be able to help me make sense out of my life? To help me find some kind of meaning in the midst of the craziness?

I arrived at the crowded suite about eight in the evening. "She is good!" a balding man exclaimed to several people crunched together on the couch. "She told me things about myself that I hadn't even put together." Twenty minutes later a young woman emerged from an inner room. "Wow!" she enthused. "She knew stuff I didn't think anyone knew! She told me exactly what I need to do when I get back home."

I'd never have put up with the cramped little room, blue with smoke, except for my desperate need and the enthusiasm of the psychic's patrons. *Had I finally found answers?* Nine o'clock. Ten. Eleven. My hopes rose with each enthusiastic patron's exit, then waffled with despair. Shortly after midnight my turn finally came.

The psychic, an attractive woman, probably in her early thirties, examined my palms. Her smile disappeared and furrows dug into her forehead. "You're having disruption in your life," she stammered. "Ah . . . with your job."

"That's true," I said. "Just got fired."

She nodded affirmatively, but the question furrows still creased her brow.

"But that's not the biggest problem," I said.

"Right. Your marriage."

"My wife just asked for divorce and I can't figure out why. Can you tell me why? And what can I do?"

She turned my hands over, then turned palms up again. The sparkle had evaporated from her eyes. She looked as troubled as I felt.

"There's no reason," she finally murmured. She paused, staring at my palms with a strange look of puzzlement. "It doesn't make sense. It shouldn't have happened. Not with your job. Not with your wife. It's just not right. It doesn't make sense." She shook her head as though bewildered.

A clock ticked, loud in the silence. Finally, she shook her head and spoke again. "She wasn't supposed to do that. It's not in the cards. It doesn't make sense. I don't know what to tell you. It shouldn't have happened."

She sat back, closed her eyes, and waited in silence for some time. "I'm just not receiving anything. I don't understand it." She waited, silent again, her eyes still closed. "I do know it wasn't supposed to happen, but I'm not getting the reason why."

She opened her eyes, then shook her head. "There is no reason. And I can't see anything you can do to help."

We talked a bit more. "Maybe I'll take my dog and go stay with my mom for a while," I suggested.

"That would be wise for you now," she agreed.

I stood to go.

Confusion was still written all over the psychic's face. And compassion. She looked like a tear might roll down her cheek any minute. She stood too. "I'm sorry."

My last hope had just collapsed. As I walked away, confusion muddled my mind. The psychic's words echoed within me like a shout in an empty cave—"There is no reason. And I can't see anything you can do to help. . . . There is no reason. And I can't see anything you can do to help. . . ." Depression dropped me into a huge cavern. It seemed there was no exit, no light, no food or water, and no one knowing or even caring that I was doomed.

Have I done something so awful that God won't even speak to me? I wondered. *Was it in this life or an earlier life? Where can I find sense?*

Falling for a Lie

Back home, I dialed the telephone. "Mom, would you consider taking in a man and a dog for a while?"

"Anytime."

At least I can expect a smile and a hug when I get there.

I telephoned the country music station manager who'd offered me a job while we were both at the Nashville seminar. "I'd really like to take the job, but I have to decline."

"Jay, we were looking forward to your coming. Our philosophies of how to run a country station would meld perfectly. What could we do on this end to make our offer more attractive to you?"

"Nothing. Really. Your offer is great. I just simply have to take some time off. Personal reasons. Things you can't do a thing about."

"Are you sure?"

"Yes. I have to be."

"If you change your mind, would you give me a call to see if I've filled the position yet?"

"Be glad to."

"We'd really like to have you."

I wanted to change my mind. It was a great opportunity. But neither my body nor mind had the energy to be productive.

As soon as I hung up the phone, I crammed clothes and personal items into a suitcase and a few boxes. Rain poured while I packed the Cherokee, loaded a box springs and mattress onto the top, and tarped and tied the roof load. When I went inside the apartment to recheck, I saw only the things I'd meant to leave for Keyli—the furniture, the TV, the kitchen supplies, everything except my personal things and one of the single beds from the guest room—I would need a place to sleep.

"Well, can I have one last hug?" I asked.

Keyli eyed me like I'd asked her to rob a bank. She held her arm out as if to hold me away. "No."

"OK." I headed out the door, then turned back. "Good-bye."

"Bye," she responded in a strained voice.

"God, where are you when I need you?" I asked aloud as the city disappeared from my rear view mirror. "Is life just a mean trick?"

The only answer was the swish of windshield wipers slashing back and forth against the storm outside.

Rain or snow poured most of the eight hundred miles to Everett, Washington, just north of Seattle. Wet to the skin and cold to the bone when I started, I couldn't seem to get warm, even with the heater blasting on high and Inki snuggled on my lap the whole trip. I shivered, sneezed, and felt like throwing up. My head pounded. My joints ached.

When Mom opened the door, she gasped. Wide-eyed, she stepped back and held onto the wall as if she might faint.

"I've gotta go to bed," I stammered.

"I'll help you get your things."

"Let's just get the bed tonight. The rest can wait."

"But . . ."

"I just can't do anymore. I don't care if everything gets stolen."

Three days cured the worst of the flu. Then the questions pummeled my numbness nonstop.

Why didn't the spirits just let me die when I was thirty?

Why is this happening to me? What am I doing wrong? For what negative karma am I paying? All I ever wanted was a little happiness. A reason to live. To make some kind of sense out of life.

I was a wreck physically as well as mentally and spiritually. No exercise. The busy-ness had crowded out jogging years ago. My weight had crept from 220 to 250. Not an ounce of it muscle. My favorite food was chocolate chip cookies—thirty or forty at a time.

Falling for a Lie

Vegetables? They were for rabbits. Fruit? Forget it. Give me anything in the two major food groups—chocolate and sugar. But even they didn't taste good anymore.

I felt dead inside. Like a zombie. I hurt. And yet I didn't care. Didn't care about myself. About my belongings. About anything or anyone. Didn't care whether I or anyone else lived or died.

In fact, I wished for a heart attack . . . or anything from outside myself that would end the pain. I didn't have the nerve to slit my wrists or jump off a tall building. I didn't have a gun.

For weeks I lay in bed with the drapes drawn. Mom tried to tempt me with her home cooking. I ate little. Occasionally I slipped into the living room to be sociable. Five minutes was about tops before I'd collapse back into bed.

After several weeks, Mom tried to interest me in something—television, magazines, job hunting. I had no interest. She encouraged me. I couldn't take it to heart. She cajoled me. I couldn't care less.

In desperation, one day I telephoned Nancy, my numerologist friend in Cleveland. "Could you help me check the numbers in my life?"

"Sure. What's going on?"

I told her about Keyli. She gasped. "No! It can't be!"

"I wish it wasn't!" I responded.

She asked questions and calculated the numbers. "I can't figure out what's going on!" she finally exclaimed with disbelief. "That's not in the numbers! You and Keyli are a perfect match!"

Nancy figured varying combinations of numbers and puzzled over them. "I can't figure out why Keyli left. But I do see one thing."

"Yes?"

"Keyli's numbers indicate she could be more vulnerable in April than at any other time. If you visualize her with you and take steps in April, you may be able to force her back to you with psychic tools."

Chapter Sixteen

Finding Love, Finding Work

Keyli? Vulnerable in April?

Both Nancy and the psychic in Nashville assured me there was no reason for our breakup. I'd seen visualization accomplish unbelievable things. Should I use psychic tools to get Keyli back?

I had used visualization. But I had made a choice about it and other similar techniques because of the very word Nancy used— force. I was totally uncomfortable with the idea of forcing someone else to function in certain ways. No matter how bad it hurt, I would not use coercion. It wouldn't be fair.

Even if I could force Keyli to come back to me, I couldn't force her to love me. Love is only love if it's given freely.

"God," I prayed, "don't ever let me get so desperate that I'd take advantage of someone else's weakness."

One afternoon as I lay in bed with Inki snuggled close beside me, a vision came. I was falling through blackness. I just kept falling and falling . . . and falling. Finally I fell through a trap door.

Falling for a Lie

Am I nearing the bottom? Will life turn around for me? Is there a tomorrow worth living for?

More days dragged by. I finally decided I couldn't take it any longer. I had read and heard about an experience people who believe in reincarnation call a "walk-in." If you're tired of living in your body, you can give it up and let another soul occupy it. Your soul walks out, another one walks in and takes over. Old body, new person. The new soul gets to live in a human body without wasting the years of growing through childhood.

Exhausted and miserable, I prayed, "God, I just can't take it anymore. Please get me out of here. Please let my soul go back to whatever plane of existence it's destined for. Please give my body to some soul that will put it to good use."

After I prayed for a walk-in, I still just laid there in bed as miserable as before. *Why me? What am I doing wrong? Why is everything going wrong in my life? Why'd I get fired again? Why this last divorce? What's wrong with me? Why are people always rejecting me?*

One afternoon, several weeks later, I mulled the same questions for the hundred-and-sixty-three-millionth time. *Why'd I get fired in Cleveland?*

Sure I made some mistakes. Said some things I shouldn't have said. Lost my temper two or three times and that was two or three times too many. But I also did a lot right. No matter how I weighed the issues, I couldn't come up with any reasons worthy of firing. If nothing else, it would surely have been worth management's trouble to say, "We've got a problem here. What can we do to smooth out this situation?"

All of a sudden it felt like a massive light exploded in my head. Like a voice said, "You're not responsible for other people's mistakes!"

Not responsible? I questioned.

I sat up in bed. Inki looked up with questioning eyes—she hadn't seen me move that quickly in months. "I'm not responsible for other people's mistakes?" I questioned softly. Inki's ears popped up.

The thought rolled around in my mind like a soccer ball in the surf. Suddenly other thoughts—thoughts totally foreign to my recent thinking—flooded over me. *Other people make choices too! Maybe management made some mistakes too! Maybe some of these things weren't my negative karma at all! Maybe somebody else's karma was working against me! Maybe I'm not always to blame for every little thing that happens to me.*

I reviewed my time at Cleveland. I should have been more tactful in telling the new manager I didn't like an idea. He should have given me some respect for what I had accomplished. I should not have lost my temper. On and on I went . . . not blaming either the manager or myself.

Relief flooded over me. I spoke aloud again, "I'm not responsible for others' mistakes. It wasn't my fault."

Inki sat up and wagged her tail.

"It wasn't my fault!" I got up, looked in the mirror, and told my image, "I'm not responsible for others' mistakes. It wasn't my fault!"

At that moment, a tiny burst of hope surged into my mind. Tiny bits of energy began to course through my body. That evening, instead of praying for a walk-in as I'd done nightly for weeks, I considered the possibility that life was going to get better. "God," I prayed, "about that walk-in . . . never mind."

Reality began to creep in. My mother's occasional reminders—"You've got to get a job, Jay"—made sense for the first time in nearly two months. At first, I'd shower and shave, go to one potential employer, then come home and collapse into bed, exhausted. My stamina increased as I proceeded.

One afternoon I received another vision. In it, I stood in front of a huge wooden door, similar to the type I'd seen pictured at the entrance to medieval castles. The door looked to be at least thirty feet tall. It had two large circular door knockers. My face was almost against the door, but it would not open.

The vision frustrated me. I had just begun to see a glimmer of hope. *Is the vision telling me the doors I want to go through will never open for me? Will I never realize my hopes?*

Over the next several days, the vision came to me repeatedly. Each time, I sank deeper into confusion and frustration. *Will all my dreams always be beyond a giant door I can't push open?*

Then it came again, only this time I received an impression along with it. "You're almost there."

Almost where? I wondered.

I didn't know. But the glimmer of hope born of realizing that perhaps not everything that happened to me was my fault encouraged me to look to the future.

First I searched for radio programming or announcing jobs. Every station in the greater Seattle area, it seemed, had long-term employees in those positions or had just hired someone. I checked out jobs from assembly lines to sales clerking. But twenty years in radio hadn't prepared me for anything else. Then, remembering that radio station owners looking for managers often wanted someone with sales experience, I decided to look for radio sales jobs.

KRKO Everett needed a salesperson. Wednesday the manager told me what he had to offer and sent me home so we could both think about it for a week. By Thursday evening I'd evaluated the situation. I knew I wanted the job. *If I'm going to be in sales*, I told myself, *I've got to ask for the order.* So I spruced up first thing Friday morning, went to the station, and asked to speak with the manager.

"Good morning, Mr. Brown."

"Good morning, Jay. I didn't expect to see you this soon."

"I know. But I've decided I would indeed like the sales work you spoke of, and I came to ask for the job."

Surprise crossed his face. He leaned back in his chair then smiled. "I like that kind of spunk. How about starting Monday?"

"Monday will be fi . . ."

"Oops," he interrupted me. "This Monday's Memorial Day. How about Tuesday."

Start Tuesday I did.

KRKO proved to be an aggressive, fun, promotional-minded station. And I learned many helpful lessons.

One of the benefits of the job was a membership at the YMCA. Ten years earlier, I used to jog up to six and a half miles at a time. My 220 pounds were muscular, lean on my six-foot-five frame. But those days were long past. My muscles and stamina had all but disappeared. Each ounce of muscle I lost was replaced with two of flab. The pounds had sneaked on . . . one chocolate chip at a time. When I first started swimming at the Y, I couldn't make it across the pool without stopping once or twice to catch my breath.

But I kept swimming, kept pushing myself. Before long I could make a full length without stopping. Then two. Then three. Eventually I swam sixty lengths quite comfortably. I didn't worry about my weight. But as I exercised, the extra weight slipped away too. Before long I felt 800 percent better physically than I'd felt in years. But I still longed for spiritual guidance and direction. *What would tomorrow bring?*

One morning a local church pastor telephoned the station about possibly doing some advertising. The receptionist gave me the information, and I called the pastor for an appointment.

Falling for a Lie

The church looked like any traditional church, but I didn't relate its name to any church I'd heard of before. The pastor wanted to reach out to the community by radio. As we talked, I noticed he possessed some unusual insights. Since I was always looking for insight, I asked him about his beliefs.

"We believe God is not pleased by narrow opinions about who He is. We need to accept people as they are and allow each one to determine how the God in them directs. Each person can commune with God himself. He can look to past lives. He can look to the future. He can know because of God in him. . . . "

The pastor could hardly have helped from seeing my interest. "Why don't you join us for services Sunday morning?" he invited.

When I walked through the door the next Sunday morning, I was enfolded in acceptance. I was greeted repeatedly, not formally, but as if the different individuals were genuinely pleased to meet me. The singing was pleasant, the meditation was comfortably familiar—almost like hypnosis, the sermon was inspiring, the ambiance was love. *This is where I belong,* I told myself.

The minister had announced that the bookstore would be open immediately after the service, so I followed a crowd there. I wandered the aisles in amazement. All of the clairvoyants were there. And everything you could ever want from New Age authors. You could choose from subjects like self-hypnosis, Buddhist philosophies, visualization, the REAL life of Christ (as opposed to the one shown in the Bible), predictions of the future, reincarnation, time warp, prophets—not the biblical kind—channeling, numerology, steps to take for world peace, self-help through the use of the occult, and many more.

I didn't see a Bible in the bookstore. It didn't matter. I had grown beyond it. I could learn more advanced wisdom through these updated, mind-expanding, and vastly more interesting books.

I attended church services every week. Even Bible study on Wednesdays, except we never used a Bible. We used a book centering on the soul and its life between bodies. *The members here must have all grown beyond the Bible,* I surmised. I thoroughly enjoyed reading the material and participating in the discussions. After the long depression, I was eager to learn and do every thing I could to override past negative karma.

Pastor Joe and I often had even deeper discussions after the meetings. One evening he shocked me. "Jay," he said, "you ought to be a minister."

"Me?" I asked, dumbfounded. I'd considered about every other line of work ever imagined—being a minister had never entered my mind.

"Yes, you," he responded. "You have insight. You think deeply. You're willing to study and grow. You communicate well. I believe that one day you'll be a minister."

"I don't know."

"Think about it. Whenever you're ready, I'll get an application from the seminary I attended. And I'll write you a great recommendation."

I didn't know about becoming a minister, but I was certain that in all my life I had never seen a group of people so loving and caring. After all the rejection I'd experienced, I reveled in the friendliness, the acceptance, the unconditioaal love.

Several months later a friend I'd worked with eight years earlier in Johnson City telephoned from Waverly, Tennessee. He'd purchased a radio station several years ago. "Jay, I need a general manager here."

I felt like I might explode with excitement. I enjoyed my job in sales, but management was what I really wanted to do. Still I was worried: *I can handle the technical part of the job. Can I do my job*

Falling for a Lie

and get along with the employees?

I'd loved Tennessee—to go back would feel like going home. I'd miss my church . . . but I was pretty mature in my understanding of reincarnation. Maybe there'd be a New Age church in Tennessee. And even if there wasn't, surely I could find someone else with whom to fellowship.

Then another offer in management came. When my friend in Waverly realized he could lose out, he started adding incentives—an occasional weekend in Nashville, a slip for my boat at the marina, and "Hey, if you come here you can bring Inki to work with you." Take Inki to work? That benefit tipped the decision toward Waverly.

When I resigned from my job in sales, Mr. Brown said, "Jay, I'm sure glad I took a chance on you."

Took a chance? That caught my attention.

"A friend of mine," he continued, "who manages a station in Seattle told me, 'Programmers just don't make salesmen! Don't hire him! I've tried it several times. It NEVER works!'

"But you just seemed to have the pluck you'd need. You learned fast, and you did well. In fact, you've been one of my top salespeople. We're going to miss you." He stood and offered his hand. "I wish you well, Jay. You've got a lot of talent. You'll do a great job!"

Inki and I headed cross-country in a packed-to-the-hilt Jeep Cherokee, towing the boat. Since Cleveland, the boat had only been out of storage long enough for moves from one community to another. I looked forward to getting it back in the water.

I pondered the challenge ahead. How would I approach it? I'd not storm in and change everything from A to Z. That tended to launch both employees and listeners into orbit. Besides, every area and every station was different. Recognizing the uniqueness of lo-

Finding Love, Finding Work

cal tastes had been part of the secret of my successes.

As usual when I arrived in a managerial position at a new station, I'd spend some time looking and listening . . . closely. Then I'd start with a glaring problem and we'd do what was necessary. When that change was implemented and most everyone was getting comfortable with it, we'd move on to another.

The needs would be somewhat different here from many of the places I'd been. WVRY - FM, known as V-105, was a satellite station. It received the main programming—music and announcers—from another area through a satellite network. Then we rebroadcast it along with local news, weather, and commercials.

Since V-105 was a 50,000-watt station, I was able to pick it up when I was still a couple hours from Waverly. The Rolling Stones rocked to life. I listened to the announcer between songs. The satellite feed sounded good. I hoped the local handled their part well. As always, I wouldn't put up with complacency. We would be the best we could be.

I listened to the '50's to '70's oldies for several miles. Then a staticky silence filled the space after the end of a song. I glanced at the radio knob as if it had turned by itself. Finally a voice came on, "You're listening to . . ." Before the announcer was done speaking, the Beatles' beat and lyrics began competing with him ". . . V-105 in Waverly."

"Hm-m-m-m," I groaned.

Inki cocked her head my way. Her ears popped up.

"Sounds like there's room for improvement."

Chapter Seventeen

Just in Case

"I'm glad to be with you here at V-105," I said during the first staff meeting. "You have a good station. But we're going to take it higher. That means excellence. You and I can make V-105 sound as professional as any station coming out of Nashville. Sure, we'll all have to stretch our skills. But we can do it if we pay attention to details.

"And, speaking of details . . . "

Cleaning up transitions back and forth between the satellite network and the local news, weather, and commercials was my first priority. We discussed setting up for the next break immediately after the last; not leaving the control room during shifts, even when the network was playing; and the importance of timing every break to the second. The philosophy of professionalism didn't sound bad. Putting it into practice presented a few complications.

Rick scowled. "What do you mean, do it over?"

"Just that. Do it over. Rewrite the commercial till it fits in thirty seconds," I answered.

"But I've already spent half an hour on this lousy thirty-second commercial."

"It's not a thirty-second commercial yet. Cut it till it is."

"It's o-o-only thirty-seven seconds."

"But seven seconds extra will muddy the transition back to the network. If we're going to sound professional, a thirty-second commercial needs to be just that—thirty seconds."

"I've tried everything!" he wailed. "I can't cut it anymore."

"Let's take a look."

Before long, we'd pared one sentence and made a couple other word changes. He read the whole thing over again. "All right, all right. You win," Rick conceded. "It'll fit thirty seconds and . . ." He smirked and rolled his eyes. ". . . and it's stronger now than it was before." He grinned and headed for the production room to re-record the commercial.

Some employees caught a glimpse of the potential of V-105 and got excited about sounding professional. Others just put in their time, took out their paychecks, and dubbed me "Mr. Perfect."

So be it. I'm good at what I do. The owner of the station knows it. Some of the employees have figured it out already, and the rest will.

But there's more to management than personal excellence. I had figured out what the station needed. But I still hadn't mastered the art of inspiring employees to *want* to do what's best for the company.

The word *personable* nagged at my mind. I worked at it. At least once or twice a day, I pulled myself away from the computer and my own work and wandered among the other employees. "How are the sales going?" I might ask of the salesperson. "How was your weekend?" "I hear your daughter was chosen as a cheerleader." I was even learning to listen.

Falling for a Lie

I hadn't been at the station long when Jennifer, the receptionist/bookkeeper, blurted, "Jay, I've got a friend you ought to meet. She's pretty, lots of fun. She'd be perfect for you."

"Thanks. But no thanks!" I exclaimed.

"But . . ."

"But nothing," I interrupted. "I've had enough of romantic relationships to last at least the rest of this lifetime! Maybe a few more."

Surprise crossed her face. She snickered. "As if you get more than one."

"I'm planning on it," I said, totally serious.

She looked at me quizzically for a long moment then grabbed the telephone log off her desk. "Did you get the message from John at the satellite network in Dallas?"

So much for her spiritual interest, I thought.

I often dropped hints about reincarnation into the station chit chat, then tried to detect an interest in spiritual things. No one nibbled.

Just days after I had arrived in Waverly, I'd scouted around for a church like the one I had enjoyed in Everett. Nothing close. But there was one with the same name in Nashville—a couple hours' drive away. *Maybe I couldn't go every week, but I could part of the time.*

An answering machine greeted me with the church name and "There's no one available to take your call at the moment, but you are important to us. Please leave your name and phone number so we can get back to you. Our services are: Sunday School at 9:30; Worship service at 11:00; and Bible study at 7:00 p.m. on Wednesdays. Bring your Bible if you can. And, remember, Jesus loves you."

Bring your Bible? Jesus loves you? I questioned. *Sounds like a traditional church.* Disappointed, I laid the receiver in its cradle.

If only there was someone with whom to share spiritual insights! I'd keep looking.

Outside of the superficial acquaintances at work, my only relationship was with my dog. Inki shadowed me everywhere—including work. She snoozed on a blanket by my office desk or tripped along unobtrusively behind me from office to control room to reception area. When the weather was comfortable, she rode along when I went on sales calls. I figured that anyone who'd stick by a person in the worst of times—like she had by me—deserved to be pampered.

"If he'd treat a woman half as good as he treats his dog," some of the employees joked, "he'd still be married to his first wife." Maybe so. But I wasn't about to take any chances.

When loneliness hit, I just worked more. There was always plenty to do. Besides hiring and training the sales and air staff, I did some of the selling, did some air work, and provided general management. I buried myself in the job—usually seven days a week, sixty or seventy hours a week. More sometimes.

Rick stepped into my office one afternoon. "Do you remember hearing about Annette?"

How could I help but remember? Annette had worked at V-105 before I arrived. Sales staff begged me to rehire Annette to write commercials—"She did a fantastic job!" Announcers told me Annette would be a good person to consider if we ever needed anyone else at the control board. The receptionist said, "Annette worked hard. She was always professional, always pleasant. She was such a delight to have around." And customers asked, "Can Annette tape this commercial?" The only crack in the list of glowing recommendations was one person who growled, "About Annette, don't get any ideas about hiring her. She's nothing but trouble. She'll call the last minute and say she's not coming to work. Or just not show up. She's undependable." I'd pondered the contradiction.

"Yes," I replied, "I remember hearing about Annette."

"Well, she's out here. She just stopped in to say 'Hello' to everyone. While she's here, why don't you come meet her?"

Curious, I jumped at the chance to meet this "saint" of V-105. She was talking to Jennifer as we approached. She was short. Wavy, auburn hair cascaded to her hips. Her voice was strong and clear.

Rick spoke. "Annette."

She turned toward him. "Hi, Rick."

A light sprinkle of freckles across her nose and cheeks hinted of little-girl innocence, yet her smile shone with a warmth gained through experience.

"This is Jay Christian, our new manager," Rick continued.

She offered her hand. "Nice to meet you."

"Nice to meet *you*," I returned. "I've heard lots of good reports about your work here."

She smiled again. Her eyes snapped. "I enjoyed working here."

We talked briefly before I headed back to my office. *Good radio voice,* I thought. *Very pleasant. And she seems intelligent and professional. Given the repeated recommendations, I'll have to keep her in mind—just in case.*

"Just in case" arrived sooner than I expected. Just a few weeks later, the Sunday afternoon board operator told me he was taking another job. Who could fill the bill?

I dialed the telephone. "Good morning, Annette. This is Jay Christian at V-105."

"Good morning."

"Our Sunday afternoon control board operator just accepted another job. I'm looking for someone who can run the board from 1:00 to 7:00 Sunday afternoons and who could also record commercials and help with remote broadcasts. Would something like that be of interest to you?"

At the interview three days later, we discussed Annette's experience, her skills, and the times she could and could not work. She could work 1:00 to 7:00 on Sunday afternoons, but she clearly stated times she could not work because of her other job and times she would not work because of her religious convictions.

I told her my plans for improving the professionalism at the station and let her know my expectations. She asked intelligent questions and indicated an interest in improving her skills.

Annette started to leave then turned back. "I thoroughly enjoy radio," she said, her amber eyes sparkling. "I'd really like the job."

Again, I was impressed with Annette's voice. *Excellent air potential!* I thought. But I questioned having to schedule radio time around her other job and around her church and other religious commitments. "I'll work anytime I can," she'd said. But, though tactful in stating her convictions, she'd made it clear that God came first.

Well, who else is there? Previous advertising hadn't turned up much potential air talent in this town of 4500. *Could Annette work out?* I wondered.

I stared at the wall in front of my desk. *She hasn't had much training, but she seems to have talent. I can train her if she's willing to learn, and she seems to be. In fact, kind of seems like a radio diamond in the rough. Her lack of training really isn't a problem.*

The question is, will we be able to work around her schedule limitations? I leaned on my elbow. *If we don't hire someone, I'll be adding those hours to **my** work week.*

I straightened up in my chair and dialed the telephone. "Annette?"

"Yes."

Falling for a Lie

"Jay Christian at V-105. Can you start next Sunday at 1:00?"

"I'll be there."

She trained Thursday. Notebook in hand, she took detailed notes on how to operate the control board, how to place the commercials and weather in the proper order, how to control the transmitters, what to do in emergencies, and much more.

Will she be here when she's supposed to work alone? I wondered. Then another thought struck. *If she does show up, considering that religion is important enough to her to risk a job over, I'll check out her spiritual interest.*

Whatever, given the second opinion about Annette's reliability, I'll stay at the station next Sunday until after her scheduled arrival . . . just in case.

Chapter Eighteen

Shifting on Axis

Sunday afternoon a car door slammed in the parking lot. I glanced at my watch: 12:45. Shortly the station door squeaked open then closed. Steps led toward the control room.

"Hi, Annette," the morning announcer greeted. "Hey! It's great to have you back!"

Whew. *My newest employee did show up! Even on time!*

I went out in the hall and greeted Annette. I mentioned a fairly new FCC rule. She double-checked a couple things about format. "I'll be in my office if you need anything," I told her. "Feel free to come get me anytime."

"Thank you. I'm glad someone will be around in case I get in a bind."

I disappeared into my office. The last thing a new employee needed was the boss standing around watching her work!

But I did listen to the radio signal as I planned my week. Her first break was clean. Then several more. *Time for a deserved compliment.*

129

Falling for a Lie

Annette looked up when I poked my head in the control room.

"Congratulations! You're doing a great job on the breaks."

Her eyes widened. "Well, thank you," she stammered.

"Just relax. You're doing fine. If you need anything, you know where I'll be."

A little after 5:00 I dropped into the control room again. "How's it feel by now to be back on the board?"

"Good." Annette smiled and looked back at the control board. "I feel kind of rusty, but it's coming back."

"You're doing a good job."

Page 130

She scrunched her nose and shook her head. "But I have so much to learn."

"It'll come in time. And we'll spend some more time in training."

"I'm planning to go on learning for a lot of centuries. Guess I shouldn't expect to master everything about radio in my first day back at work."

Her comment caught me by surprise. *Lot of centuries? What's she mean?* "Like in another lifetime?" I asked.

"Yeah, you could say it that way."

I caught a glimpse of the clock. "Oops. I'd better get out of your way so you can be ready for the next break. You're doing so well you don't need anyone looking over your shoulder. I'm going to take off . . . if you feel comfortable."

"Yeah, I think I'll be OK."

"Great. See you next week.

Too bad the "another lifetime" discussion didn't come up earlier, I thought as I climbed into my Jeep. *Looks like there may be an opportunity for some spiritual fellowship yet.*

Just the possibility of talking about spiritual things with another human excited me. When I arrived home, I meditated, then immersed myself in a new book. It predicted that around the turn of the century cataclysmic changes would usher in a new age of peace. The predictions of the earth shifting on its axis and resultant weather changes and natural catastrophes fascinated me.

Frankly, some days it seemed like the station had already shifted on its axis and it might self-destruct any minute. Often when I communicated instructions, I double- and triple-checked to be sure the recipients understood. Still, practically before Inki could turn around, someone would be doing just the opposite of what I'd told them.

Like one morning when the control room was empty . . . again. Dale didn't seem to remember "Stay" as well as Inki did.

"Where's Dale?" I asked Jennifer.

She looked up from a column of figures. "I don't know. Isn't he in the control room?"

"Not unless he just became invisible."

I looked in the production room. There he sat, taping a commercial. I snapped open the door. "Somehow, I get the idea you're not at the control board."

He punched the recorder off. "Just taping a couple commercials in between things," he drawled.

"Is your next break set up?"

"Not yet. I'll get to it in a minute."

"Have you checked the clock lately?"

He looked up at the clock, then exploded out of his chair and in to the control board. Hands, tapes, and knobs flew. Information from the satellite network meant only for the station staff was broadcast to much of middle and western Tennessee, then cut off mid-word as a local commercial started. Dale cut the last commercial short and still blundered into the middle of a song as he rejoined the network.

When the network played again, he sighed and wiped his hand across his forehead. "Boy, I blew that one."

"I'd agree with your assessment," I said. "Any idea why?"

"I just didn't watch the clock close enough. I'll watch better after this."

"Do you remember us talking about not leaving the control room during a shift?" I asked.

"Yeah, but there's time sometimes to cut a commercial."

"Was there this time?"

"I just wasn't watching close enough."

"And a bunch of other times you weren't watching closely enough either. Right?"

"Well . . . yeah. I'll watch closer."

"How about you just following the new policy of staying at the control board when it's your shift?"

So much for excellence!

Excellence seemed absent in my spiritual life as well. As little or much as I practiced self-hypnosis or meditated or read, I didn't seem to be getting any answers from within myself or from spirits that could guide me.

Maybe the minister in Everett was right, I considered, one evening as I meditated. *Maybe I ought to get out of radio and go to seminary. Maybe if I were a minister, I'd be closer to God.*

I dialed the telephone. "Pastor Joe, I've been thinking about what you said about my becoming a minister . . . "

"Jay, I knew it!" he enthused. "I just knew you would!"

He gave me the address and phone number for the seminary. I telephoned the next day. Several days later, I noted the return address on a large envelope from my mailbox. Standing on the porch, I ripped into the packet and began reading. Academic requirements—*I'll make that.* Cost—*It'll be a scramble if I can get that much money together by mid-September.* References—*Pastor Joe promised me a good one.* Deadline—. My heart sank.

If I had been just a day or two late, I'd have pushed to have them consider me. Records and applications could be faxed. But . . .

I went inside and plopped onto the ugliest orange love seat that any furniture manufacturer had ever thought up. Desperate for furniture, I'd bought it and the rest of my furniture at a motel used-furniture sale. The love seat wasn't particularly comfortable, but it had been cheap.

I looked at the application again—"Final date for consideration as a student: July 10." I glanced at today's date—August 16.

"God," I said, "I thought I'd finally found what was right for me. But it's not working out any better than most things I've tried in the last few years. Is it the wrong thing? Or . . . maybe . . . just the wrong timing?"

Well . . . I could stand most anything for a while. This year I'd give the station every ounce of energy I had. I'd save money, get all the records and references I needed, and have my application into the seminary at least four months early for next year.

But for now, back to work. There were policies to be evaluated, announcers to communicate with, salespeople to train, sales to do myself, schedules to adjust, research to do, customers with whom to arrange remote broadcasts, commercials to tape, ball games to find sponsors for, technical adjustments to make, and a new announcer to train.

Chapter Nineteen

Mission

One Tuesday afternoon at the station, Annette arrived in the middle of a disagreement between Ben, one of our salesmen, and Mike, one of our announcers. She walked through the door with a smile in her voice. "Hi, guys. It's a beautiful day. What's up?"

Silence.

She turned to Jennifer. "Is Jay in?"

"Yeah, he's back in his office."

"You in trouble too?" Mike sneered.

Annette chuckled. "Don't think so," she answered. "Just coming for evaluation and training. And I'm glad. I like radio. I'd like to learn to be a really good announcer."

I'd moved to the salesroom door. As Annette walked through the room, I could almost feel the ice melting. Mike's arm dropped. The finger he'd been jabbing at Ben relaxed. The furrows in Ben's forehead softened. And Jennifer, in the middle of most everything that happened in this small building, heaved a sigh of relief.

"Good afternoon, Annette," I greeted. "Come on back."

She did. And Mike and Ben continued their discussion more softly and sanely.

I'd noticed before that Annette seemed to be surrounded by an aura of peace. Just her presence had a quiet, positive influence.

Seated in the office, I complimented Annette on her promptness and on perfectly timed, clean breaks back and forth from network to our local station when she was running the control board. "Have you ever been told you're too perfect?" I asked.

She laughed. "No. I've been told I had a lot of problems, but never that one!"

"Well, let me be the first."

She crinkled her brows. Question marks were written all over her face.

She looked so puzzled I couldn't help but chuckle. "It's like this," I explained. "Sometimes when a person focuses really hard to make every word clear and understandable on radio, they overenunciate. The biggest thing I'd like you to work on is simply to relax. Just relax and sound natural."

In the production room, I gave her some weather reports to read and worked with her to help her sound over the radio like she was telling listeners about the weather, not reading it to them. She made strides forward.

"I can tell the difference," she marveled. "What's my next lesson going to be?"

"This is the big lesson for now," I replied. "You're getting the technical part down pat, and that will help you stay relaxed. But for now, just relax when you read the weather or cut a commercial."

The next Sunday, as usual, I showed up at the station mid-morning. Even though Annette excelled in her work, I still started getting nervous about noon. Would she call in sick today? Would she just not show up? Undependable employees are a nuisance anyplace, but in an on-air radio job, you can't just wait and do the work the next day. Someone *has* to be there.

When I heard a car door slam from the parking lot about 12:45, I heaved a sigh of relief . . . again. *One more Sunday afternoon I don't have to do the air shift,* I thought, *though I'm not sure it matters too much. Except for self-hypnosis, meditation, or reading about reincarnation or the coming new age, about all I do at home is rot in front of the TV and skarf down pop, cookies, and chocolate.*

As usual during an operator's time at the control board, I dropped in and chatted a bit while the network played. With Annette, I was especially curious about what made most everyone think she was wonderful and one person think she was awful. I'd never been around anyone like her. Even when everything was going wrong, she exuded a calmness that was foreign to my thinking. One day, early in her employment at the station, I had asked her, "Are you acquainted with karma?"

"Some," she responded. "How do *you* view karma?"

What an invitation! I launched into an explanation. She listened and asked questions along the way. We discussed spiritual issues from week to week. Her views were definitely from a more traditional religion, yet she seemed interested in what I believed. She never condemned me. And she asked questions that made me think.

I began to look forward to our Sunday afternoon discussions. The spiritual fellowship often felt like the highlight of my week. Perhaps she'd share my reincarnation beliefs eventually.

Suffering was one issue for which I'd never found any answers in traditional religion. "Have you noticed all the disasters lately?" I asked Annette one afternoon.

"Yes! And all over! From Mt. St. Helens blowing her top in

Washington, to the earthquake in Mexico City, to famines in Ethiopia and Sudan."

"And the eruption of Pinatubo in the Philippines," I added.

"And one hurricane after the other across the southern United States."

I shook my head, then sighed. "Seems like the last few years the news has been full of snowstorms and rainstorms, floods and mud slides, record high temps and record lows, tornadoes, and tropical storms. Sometimes I wonder if we're already beginning to see the catastrophic events that Edgar Cayce predicted for around the year 2000."

Most everyone thought I was crazy for even bringing up such things. But Annette seemed to think we'd see even more and worse catastrophes. "Remember the author I told you about, the one that some people consider to have had a prophetic gift?"

"Yeah."

"I have a book she wrote that you might like to read. In the last few chapters she deals with exactly what we're talking about. Those chapters fascinated me. I checked out the Bible references it gives and have come to think of those chapters as a chronicle of events that will probably happen on this old earth in the fairly near future. Want me to bring it so you can read it?"

"Sure."

I knew from previous discussions that any book Annette would be recommending would most likely come from more traditional religious thinking than I usually considered. But the modern enlightenment fascinated me. Besides, I figured, the more I absorbed now about all kinds of religions, the better prepared I'd be to find answers at the seminary next year and to eventually help others accept the greater truth that reincarnation helps one understand.

"Start here at the marker," Annette said when she brought the

Falling for a Lie

book, "These last seven chapters are about the catastrophes and other events we were talking about."

Eager, that evening I switched off the Christmas specials on TV, curled up in the ugly orange love seat, and picked up Annette's book. "God," I prayed, "please guide me as I read." I looked at the title, *The Great Controversy Between Christ and Satan.* I opened to Annette's marker and started to read.

The next thing I knew, I woke up with a start, groggy, not knowing where I was or what was happening. I rubbed my eyes then looked around the room. *I'm home.* I glanced down and saw a book on my lap. *Oh yeah, I just started reading Annette's book.*

I stretched, then picked up the book again. A couple sentences later, I could barely keep my eyes open. I gave up reading and went to bed.

The next night, after a quick bite to eat, I picked up Annette's book. Sentences into reading, I couldn't concentrate. My eyelids drooped. I'd never taken drugs in my life, but I felt drugged. I read a couple sentences, then drifted off to sleep. After a while I woke, read a paragraph, and was gone again. Eventually, I laid the book down and pulled out the new issue of *Radio & Records* and perused it cover to cover. Still wide awake when I finished that, I picked up Annette's book again and fell asleep in the middle of the second paragraph.

When I woke, I realized that while I had slept, I'd heard voices. Not audibly, but in my head. Numerous voices. Like my head was full of many people talking all at once, very loud and unorganized. Cacophony. I couldn't understand what was being said. At least I couldn't remember it. But the noise was raucous, dissonant, unsettling.

The chapter titles and Annette's description of the book fascinated me. I wanted to read it. What was going on?

The next Sunday afternoon at work Annette asked, "Finding anything interesting in the book I loaned you?"

"Not yet." I sighed. "I must really be exhausted from work lately. I want to read it, but every time I start, exhaustion comes over me and I go to sleep."

"Do you always get sleepy when you read?" she asked.

"No. I read or meditate frequently in the evening. I've never experienced the weird grogginess that's been coming over me lately."

Annette's smile disappeared. She looked like she was thinking. She started to speak then stopped. "Maybe," she finally said, "some-one . . . or something . . . doesn't want you to read that book."

Over the next few days I realized I could read anything else late into the night, even when I'd had an exhausting day. I rarely had trouble staying awake. Especially when I read New Age books, no matter what hour of day or night, I felt energized. *What was going on?*

I usually prayed for guidance before I started reading. *Hm-m-m. What if I asked God to keep me awake while I read?*

That evening I prayed, "God, please guide my mind. And please keep me awake so I can read this book."

I turned to Annette's marker and read page after page.

How does this compare with Edgar Cayce's predictions? I asked myself over and over. I found both the similarities and the differences interesting.

As I read, night after night, sometimes the drugged-like drowsiness overcame me again. And the voices startled me. When I wakened, I prayed again.

Annette's book referred frequently to the Bible. I watched for inconsistencies, for lapses in logic, for obviously weird and unbiblical ideas. I figured finding error wouldn't be hard. All the traditional Christian ministers I'd questioned had stumbled over their own

Falling for a Lie

gospel. They said they believed the Bible. But they used verses to say things those verses obviously did not say if you just read before and after. I dropped them like I would a hot potato.

As soon as I see the error in the information Annette is sharing, I thought, *I'll drop it too. But she seems sincere. She seems totally dedicated to truth. I'll show her the error, too, and help her see the truth of reincarnation.*

Then a new thought shocked me. "God," I said aloud, "you kept me here this year so I could share with Annette, didn't you?" I smiled and patted Inki's head. "Maybe I will have converted one of these traditional Christians to the beautiful truth of reincarnation before I even get to seminary."

"God, help me see the error in the book," I prayed.

Chapter Twenty

Getting Acquainted

"Interesting reading," I told Annette when I took her book back a few weeks later.

We discussed it briefly several different times. One Sunday when she was all set up for the next break I said, "One thing I noticed in your book—Jesus got a lot of emphasis."

"Yes."

"I don't understand the way churches look at Jesus," I said. "At every church I ever went to, I got the idea Jesus was a wimp. He hung His head, turned His cheek, and never stood up for anything."

Furrows dug into Annette's forehead. She looked totally puzzled. "Jesus? A wimp?"

"Yeah. He was such a milquetoast."

"That's not the Jesus I read about in the Bible," she said.

"Me either. Jesus talked pretty straight—called hypocrites whitewashed tombstones full of dead men's bones. Even told some they were snakes . . . right to their face."

"You're right." Annette said. "Jesus was strong. And intelligent and clever and . . ."

By the end of our discussion, I shook my head. "I can't believe it! Another Christian sees Jesus the way I do! The way I always have!"

"You've *got* to read another book I have!" Annette urged. "It's by the same author as the other one I loaned you, but it's all about the life of Jesus. If you thought the other book was interesting . . . well . . . this book'll knock your socks off. You've *got* to read it, Jay."

"It's really that good?" I questioned.

"It's better than that."

"OK, OK. You've sold me. Can I borrow yours, or do I have to go buy it?"

"I'll loan you mine," she said. "I'll bring it next time I come in."

Life never got boring at the station. I did some sales on my own and spent considerable time training new salespeople. Sales presented some unique challenges since our station was regional and several smaller stations broadcast to separate communities within our market area.

"What? You want seven dollars for one commercial?" one business owner questioned. "Our local station sells me ads for a dollar a holler."

I'd heard that maneuver before. "I understand that, sir, and I hope you keep supporting your local station. They can reach many of the 3,500 people in and around your town, but we can do something they can't. We not only have a lot of listeners here, but with our 50,000 watts of power, we can reach the surrounding counties, taking the message of your business to thousands of people who are, right now, unaware of you."

Getting Acquainted

We sold some accounts. Some we didn't.

Often when I sold advertising in Clarksville, in the evening I'd go to the bookstore in the mall and look for New Age books. I'd nearly worn out my old standbys. I pretty well understood reincarnation and growth in this physical life. With stress keeping me feeling like I was wired to 220, I especially looked for the books about the new age of peace and the descriptions of the events that would usher it in. I compared the new books to the information Edgar Cayce had shared. He was the standard, as far as I was concerned.

But then there was Annette's book. Ideas from it rolled around in my mind from time to time. One of the things it talked about was peace in spite of all hell breaking loose around you. I remembered a phrase I'd heard someplace. Was it from the Bible? "The peace of God which passeth all understanding."

That kind of peace was foreign to me, for sure. When I'd arrived in Waverly for my first radio station general manager job, I was physically fit and raring to go. I had dreamed big and made plans—in short order, as long as karma smiled on me; I'd take V-105 to heights it had never known.

But what was wrong? Cooperation didn't materialize. My frustration level soared.

Peace? I pondered one afternoon at my desk. I thought about the goings on at the station and the varied people involved. "Hm-m-m," I said as I realized, *Annette's the only one around here that stays cool under every circumstance. I wonder . . . what does she know that the rest of us don't?*

"Jay," the receptionist called. "Telephone."

So much for a moment to think. I grabbed the receiver.

A few days later Annette poked her head in my office door. "Good morning. I'm headed out to help John with a remote broadcast. But here's the book I promised you."

"Thanks," I said. Then, as an afterthought, I asked, "Does it have anything to say about peace?"

Annette turned back. She smiled in her unperturbable way. "Sure does. A lot."

That evening, I turned off the TV and folded into the orange love seat with the book *The Desire of Ages*. "God, please guide me," I prayed.

I felt my eyelids getting heavy, my head nodding a time or two. The next thing I knew I woke up, groggy, with an uproar echoing in my mind. For an instant I groped to figure out where I was and what was going on. I rubbed my eyes open. *I'm home. I was reading. Annette's book! This is like before! What IS going on?*

I thought about the chapters I'd read in Annette's other book. It showed clearly from the Bible that there were two powers vying for supremacy in people's lives, in their minds. The instruction I was given when I learned about hypnosis was to always pray for protection from evil spirits.

"God," I prayed, "I don't know what's going on, but besides guiding my mind and helping me find truth, would you please protect me from evil spirits?"

I opened the book and read. And read.

In the following weeks, I always prayed for God's guidance AND protection before I began reading. Occasionally, the extreme fatigue would settle over me again. But I nearly always caught myself before I went to sleep. I would pray again and start reading. Sometimes I'd have to pray repeatedly before I could go on with the book. But as I read and prayed, the overpowering sleep tripped me up less and less.

The book on the life of Christ was fascinating. One night I caught myself pounding the arm of the love seat shouting, "This is

Jesus! That's who He is!"

Inki cocked her head and looked at me like she thought I'd lost my mind. I felt a little foolish. But this book made Jesus come alive. I felt like I was getting acquainted with Him. He lived not only in the Middle East two thousand years ago. He walked through my life in Waverly, Tennessee, U.S.A.

The Jesus I now read about was patient. Though He didn't hesitate to help hypocrites see where they stood, He never condemned an honest seeker of truth. He was not weak or weird. The principles He taught weren't dry relics of the ancient past. They were relevant to today! To my world! To me! I was getting acquainted with Jesus. And admiring Him more than I'd ever dreamed.

Whenever I had a chance to talk with Annette, we discussed the latest drama I'd been reading in the life of the strong, decisive Jesus. I'd met lots of churchgoers, but I'd never before met anyone who took the Jesus of the Bible as seriously as Annette did. The deeper our discussions, the more excited I got.

"You seem to really enjoy talking about Jesus," she said one day when I was nearly through reading the book.

"Yes, I do . . . now that I've found someone else in the world who sees Him as a real person."

"I do too. But there are others, also, who share our interest," she said. "Would you like to go to church with me sometime?"

"Go to church?" My mind raced.

From Annette's comments, it has to be more of a traditional church than I'm used to. But it surely promotes some interesting ideas. Going to church would maybe answer a lot of questions for me. Besides, I'd never yet met a preacher I couldn't stump. All I'll have to do is go once and ask a few questions. If they don't use the Bible any more carefully than the rest of the traditional Christian preachers I've ever met, I'll know they're not worth their weight in salt either. And after Annette

Falling for a Lie

sees her preacher fumbling for answers to simple questions, it will be a lot easier to share reincarnation with her.

I looked back to Annette. "Sure," I said. "I'll go to church with you."

Chapter Twenty-one

Questions Welcomed

A few days later, Annette and her college-age daughter, Cari, rode with me on the way to their church. As much as I'd enjoyed spiritual fellowship with Annette during our many discussions at the station, that morning I didn't have much to say. A variety of questions I'd asked other ministers rumbled around in my mind. I didn't even notice the landscape until Annette exclaimed, "Look! The bright green leaf buds are just starting to open."

Just beyond Lobelville we turned onto a side road and wandered a short distance past houses and small pastures. Horses reached over the fence that separated pasture from the small church. In the church foyer, several different people greeted us warmly. The service was interesting, but I was disappointed that the pastor would not be there that day because he was preaching at another church.

The man who preached referred to himself several times as a farmer. But he surely seemed to know the Bible. He turned to various texts easily—no turning to the list of the books of the Bible

Falling for a Lie

at the front like I usually had to do. And he made a lot of sense.

People seemed warm and friendly as we exited. There was lots of visiting between the others and with us. In fact, one couple invited us to their home for dinner. Turned out to be a pleasant afternoon. I couldn't help but notice that Bible verses wove in and out of conversation comfortably. Annette and this man and woman obviously spent some time with the Bible.

But I saved my tough questions till I could talk directly to the pastor. He was scheduled to be at their church the following week. I'd be doubly ready by then.

Pastor John Riggs was a small man—thin and a foot or so shorter than I. But if he lacked anything in size, he certainly didn't lack a thing in enthusiasm. And his sermon was no philosophical treatise. It was a study on salvation—straight from the Bible. I perused the verses surrounding the texts he read. Not a single one contradicted the way he applied it.

After the service, he greeted people as they left. His was no wet-dishrag handshake. This little man grasped my hand with strength. "Glad to have you here."

We visited for several minutes. I was impressed with his genuine interest and friendliness. Finally I asked, "Would you mind if I asked you a question or two about the Bible?"

"Not at all! Nothing I like better than studying and talking about the Bible. What's on your mind?"

"Well, frankly, I'm not all that sure the Bible is dependable. For instance, remember when Cain killed Abel?"

"Yeah."

"And God chased Cain away to another part of the world?"

"Uh-huh."

"And Cain married."

"Yeah."

"Adam and Eve and Cain are the only people on the earth according to the Bible. Where did Cain find a wife? And where did the people in the land of Nod come from?"

"Good question," he said with a smile. "Let me grab my Bible."

Good question? I couldn't believe it. *No minister had ever complimented my questions before. He really didn't seem to mind.*

He got his Bible, a King James Version, and we sat down in a pew.

"Cain," he said, as he opened his Bible on his lap. "That's going to be right near the beginning. Genesis." He flipped a few pages. "Here it is . . . in Genesis 4."

I turned to Genesis 4 also.

"In verse 8 it talks about Cain killing Abel," he said as he scanned. "Verse 16 talks about the land of Nod. Seventeen's about Cain's wife . . . but let's just go back to the beginning of the chapter so we see the whole picture. Is that alright? Do you have time?"

I blinked. *Huh? Did he say what I thought I heard?* That was one of the main bones I had to pick with a lot of preachers. So many with whom I'd talked before took a verse here or there, but when I read the verse in its context, it said something other than what it looked like it said just by reading the one verse. "Sure," I said. "I have time, if you do."

"Good." He shifted in the pew. "Chapter 3 ends with Adam and Eve leaving the Garden of Eden," Pastor Riggs said. We read the fourth chapter together.

"Did you see anything about the amount of time that had elapsed through the chapter?" Pastor Riggs asked when we finished reading.

"No. But there had to be enough time for Cain and Abel to grow up and for Cain to get married."

"Right. Any idea at what age they married then?"

"No."

"Look over here in Chapter 5," he said. "Verse 3—Adam lived 130 years and had a son they named Seth. Verse 4—Adam lived 800 years after he had Seth and had more sons and daughters. Verse 5—Adam lived 930 years. And as we go on down, Seth lived 105 years before he had a son then he lived on another 807 years and died when he was 912."

We looked on down through chapter 5. Everyone lived several hundred years. And what appeared to be their first children were born when the father was old by our standards.

"We really don't have any idea specifically how much time elapsed," Pastor Riggs said, "but we do know that often first children weren't born until after the father was a hundred years old. And, like verse 4 said, Adam had other sons and daughters. How many children could Adam and Eve have had during the time Cain grew up?"

"If Cain didn't have his first child till he was a hundred . . . or more, Adam and Eve could have had quite a family by then."

"You're right," Pastor Riggs said. "Since they were so close to the perfection of creation, there were no genetic problems with marrying within a family. So Cain easily could have married a sister. In fact, he may have already been married before he killed Abel. He may well have taken his wife and family with him to another part of the earth."

The whole picture unfolded to me like I'd never seen it before. "And if there was indeed only one extended family, at that point," I added, "there's all the reason in the world why Cain would have been worried about someone taking revenge. The person he killed was everyone's son, husband, father, brother, or uncle."

"Right," Pastor Riggs agreed.

"I can't believe it. I've puzzled over that for years. And the answer is all right there in the Bible if you just read the whole thing and use your head a little."

"Does it make sense now?"

"Yeah. Perfect sense."

Pastor Riggs welcomed question after question. And he answered them straight from the Bible. Finally, I asked, "Do you have time for one more question?"

"Sure."

"Well," I asked, "how can God condone adultery among His 'chosen' people in the first part of the Bible yet tell us that if we do those things, it's sin and we'll go to hell?"

"Are you thinking of any specific examples?"

"David."

"David with Bathsheba?" he asked.

"Yeah, I think that was her name."

"Did David think what he did was all right?"

I tried to remember the story, but it had been years since I'd heard it. "I don't know."

"Let's take a look." He paged through His Bible. "Maybe in Samuel?" I was still looking for Samuel when he added, "Here—Second Samuel 11 is where that incident starts."

Again, we read whole passages together. David surely wasn't announcing his affair. It didn't take long to figure out that he didn't think it was the best practice.

"But the real question is," Pastor Riggs said, "what did God think about it? Right?"

"Right."

"Let's read chapter 12."

We read the prophet's parable of a man who stole a pet lamb from his neighbor. David reacted angrily. Then the prophet announced, "Thou art the man." (verse 7) God's reaction? "Wherefore hast thou despised the commandment of the Lord, to do evil in his sight?" (verse 9) David recognized the awfulness of what he'd done. He said, "I have sinned against the Lord" (verse 13).

"God said David sinned," Pastor Riggs said, "and David recognized it as sin. Unfortunately, David wasn't much different than the rest of us. Let's look over in the New Testament at Romans 3:23."

I found it and started reading aloud: "'For all have sinned . . .'"

"How many sin?" Pastor Riggs asked.

"All."

"Everyone has sinned. Fortunately, David knew about something else. In fact," Pastor Riggs continued, "one of David's prayers after this is recorded in Psalm 51." We turned to that text. "See how his prayer starts?" he asked.

"'Have mercy upon me, O God . . .'" I read.

"David knew," Pastor Riggs interrupted, "that even though he'd committed adultery and murder and tried to cover them up, God still loved him. Look at the way he continues praying."

"'Have mercy upon me, O God, according to thy lovingkindness: according unto the multitude of thy tender mercies blot out my transgressions.'"

As we read, the text made it clear that David recognized the heinousness of his sin. But he begged God for forgiveness and cleansing.

"God doesn't belittle sin," Pastor Riggs said. "Sin costs a horrible price—death. But Jesus paid that price. Because of His death, David and Abraham and Moses, and Peter and John, and you and I all can be forgiven. In fact, let's look at Romans again—chapter 6, verse 23."

"'For the wages of sin is death; but the gift of God is eternal life through Jesus Christ our Lord.'"

"We've all sinned," the pastor said. "So we've all earned the wages of sin. And there's *nothing* we can do to earn back life. But God pleads with us not to accept that wage. He paid the death price of sin, and He has a gift for everyone who'll accept it. God's gift is life.

"It's only because of God's gift," he continued, "that David or you or I can have eternal life with God. If we could earn it ourselves, it would be salvation by works. But we can't! Salvation is God's gift—God's gift of grace." He shifted in the pew. "Just because something's in the Bible doesn't mean it's the way God wanted things to be. He recorded the Bible characters' lives, warts and all. No touch-up work to make them look perfect. That gives me hope. If God's grace is big enough to save them, it must be big enough to save me too."

"OK, so what was sin back then is still sin and vice versa. Right?"

"Right."

"But this text. . ." I pointed to Romans 6:23. "Doesn't it prove reincarnation?" I had him this time. "Everybody dies . . . whether they're good or bad. So there must be another life when those who have worked off their negative karma continue to live."

Chapter Twenty-Two

News About Hell

"Great question," Pastor Riggs said. "But let's look at that verse again. There are two phrases. Right?"

I looked back down at Romans 6:23. "Right. 'The wages of sin is death' and 'the gift of God is eternal life.'"

"What's the word that connects the two phrases?"

I looked again at the text. "But."

"What does 'but' mean?" he asked.

I pondered an instant. "'But' points out contrast."

"Exactly. If the two phrases were connected by 'and,' then if we looked at only this text, what you're saying would make sense. But they're not. 'For the wages of sin is death; *but* . . .' The 'but' tells us there's something different coming. There's a choice, essentially. '*but* the gift of God is eternal life through Jesus Christ our Lord.'"

"That's important," Pastor Riggs continued, "but that's just a tiny piece of the answer. The death Paul is talking about here is the 'second death.'"

"Second death?" I questioned. I'd never heard that phrase.

"Yes. But that study could take a while. I'm willing to go right on and study it with you now, if you want. But I think it would mean more to you if I gave you some information to study at home and then we met again and studied it together. Would you be comfortable with that?"

My stomach had already growled several times. "Sure. That's fine."

"I'm glad you're willing to study on your own," Pastor Riggs said. "I suppose that's especially important to me because of my own experience. I searched for years for truth. At first, I searched the churches. I finally found one that satisfied me.

"I became a lay preacher. I loved my church, loved my people. Further Bible study gave depth, real substance, to my beliefs. In the process, I learned to trust God. He became my friend.

"Life was wonderful . . . until I discovered truth that contradicted a doctrine my church believed." He raised an eyebrow then sighed. "I'm just human enough to have made my share of mistakes. And I've learned the best thing to do when I discover I've goofed is to admit it, make amends, and start living right. Doesn't that make sense?"

"Yeah," I agreed.

"I admitted my mistake," Pastor Riggs continued, "and proceeded to obey what God had revealed to me in the Bible. Unfortunately, my church wasn't excited about the truth I'd discovered. It was traumatic leaving the church and the people I loved. But it was worth it. Remember, Jay, it's always worth it to search for truth. It's always worth it to follow truth . . . wherever it leads you."

Pastor Riggs stood. "I'll go get the Bible study guides." He returned shortly with a handful of material. "Don't just believe me or these pamphlets. Study for yourself until you know what truth is according to the Bible."

My head was swimming. On the way home I told Annette and Cari, "I can't believe it! Years ago I asked numerous ministers most of the same questions I just asked Pastor Riggs. None of them gave me answers that satisfied.

"Pastor Riggs didn't seem the least bit bothered by *any* question I threw at him. Come to think of it, though, he really didn't answer my questions himself. He turned to the Bible. We read together. Essentially, he let the Bible answer for itself. He basically just showed me where to find the answers in the Bible."

At home I ate a quick lunch then headed west. With the hours I worked, I rarely took any time for relaxing. I'd planned to take the afternoon off and enjoy Kentucky Lake in my little-used boat. No sense letting my curiosity about the pamphlets foil my relaxing or letting my relaxing curb my curiosity.

I headed the boat south from the marina across the lake from New Johnsonville. The water was glassy, the sky nearly as blue as the lake. Rolling hills edged the lake. Dark evergreens accented the delicate, bright spring greens of deciduous trees starting to leaf out.

I found a peaceful spot near the lush shoreline and dropped anchor. No homes, no businesses, no structures of any kind. Just water, rocks, trees, and more trees. The silence always quieted my turmoil.

But that day, Inki and I lounged in the sun only a few minutes before curiosity got the best of me. I grabbed my Bible and the booklets Pastor Riggs had shared. The first pamphlet's title asked "Are the Dead Really Dead?"

I know the answer to that even if these Christians don't, I thought. *No need to dive deep into a sticky issue. They'll probably stumble on something else along the way, and I won't even have to deal with this.*

The next pamphlet's title read "Is the Devil in Charge of Hell?" I thought back over the years. Hell was the subject that made me hate God . . . until I learned about reincarnation. I was so thankful to have learned that each person gets all the chances they need to learn what's necessary to live on a heavenly plane. So grateful to have learned that God wasn't torturing people in a forever-burning hell through centuries and millennia. "So what are these traditional Christians going to say about hell?" I questioned, then started reading.

What? The Bible says no one's burning in hell now? That hell doesn't start till after the final judgment and resurrection of everyone?

So somebody that sinned five thousand years ago wouldn't have to suffer any longer than someone that sinned now. That's surely more fair than what I was taught when I was a kid.

The shrill whistle of a hawk broke the stillness. I spotted him practically straight above me, floating on the air with hardly a wing movement. He circled over the hillside then back over the shore. Captivated by his calm soaring, I watched until, eventually, he flapped wide wings and headed over the hill.

I turned back to the pamphlet. *Could this possibly be true?* I opened my Bible and looked up each text, reading several verses or a chapter or more around the verses the pamphlet quoted.

Occasionally a boat and skier flew past or fishermen heading from one fishing spot to another. They passed far out in the lake. Their wakes were so spent by the time they got to my peaceful spot that the water lapped lightly, peacefully against the shore.

I read on and on. I couldn't find anything misquoted.

Later, I looked up as another boat passed. "Wow! How'd that happen?" I questioned aloud. Inki perked up, tilting her head. "We'd better get going." The sun had dropped mighty close to the horizon.

Falling for a Lie

The inboard/outboard motor purred to life. We headed south a little farther before circling back and speeding north.

The ideas I'd been reading about still filled my mind. *Hm-m-m,* I thought when I was almost to the marina, *I don't think she'd mind.* I moored the boat, got my staff phone list from my car, and dialed the pay phone. "Annette, I've been studying the Bible all afternoon. Would you have time to answer a few questions?"

She gave me directions and I drove to her apartment on the lakeshore. We sat on the back lawn, overlooking the water. Inki sniffed, snooped, and ran circles in the large yard.

"I can hardly believe what I've been reading!" I enthused. "I guess I just want to know if I'm understanding it. If anyone else believes like this or even thinks it's possible."

"So, what have you been reading?"

"I started with a pamphlet Pastor Riggs gave me. Then I spent most the afternoon reading in the Bible."

"What were you reading about?"

"About hell. Is it true that the Bible says hell doesn't start till after everyone has died and then has been resurrected?"

"Yes. That's what I understand from the Bible."

"Do you believe that hell doesn't burn its victims throughout eternity? But it burns hot and fast, like fire in a stubble field? That in hell, those who chose to follow Satan rather than to enjoy friendship with God will experience the second death—the final death? Then that's the end of them? There's no torturing?"

"Yeah, that's what I read in the Bible," Annette agreed.

"That sounds wonderful. But doesn't the Bible talk about everlasting fire when it talks about hell?"

"Yes, it does," she answered.

"So what's that mean?"

"Well, a place or two it refers to hell. And one place, it refers to the fire that destroyed Sodom and Gomorrah."

"Sodom and Gomorrah? Those towns aren't still burning, are they?" I asked.

"No, they're not. The biblical terms *forever, eternal,* or *everlasting* can mean 'as long as a thing lasts.' An eternal fire, or an unquenchable fire burns till what it is burning is burned up—like Sodom and Gomorrah. When the fuel burns completely, the fire goes out."

"Hm-m-m." I was thinking.

"After reading all the Bible says about hell," Annette said, "my understanding is that hell's punishment is eternal, but not its punishing. Hell destroys the destruction sin has caused, then Jesus creates a new earth."

As we talked, an egret waded in the shallows. Sunset turned the sky and water pink, then purple, then deep, night blue.

I marveled aloud, "If this is what the Bible says about hell, that doesn't make God out to be an ogre."

"Not at all," Annette agreed.

"I never dreamed that hell could make God seem good and loving."

On the way home I wondered, *Could this possibly be right?* It made sense. But it was totally foreign to what I'd ever heard— either from Christians or New Age teachers.

For years now I had studied, meditated, and lived New Age. The recent Bible reading brought back memories from formative days. Evaluating the new ideas, my mind jumped back and forth between New Age and what I remembered from Christianity.

The next day, I studied hell some more. I pondered, then decided, *No need to conclude on this right now. What do those other pamphlets say?*

Evening by evening, I curled up in the orange love seat with my Bible and those pamphlets. I nearly always had a question or six for Annette when we got to talk a few minutes.

Week by week, after prayer meeting I pummeled Pastor Riggs with questions—way more questions than I'd ever asked anyone else. And harder questions than I'd ever pressed to any other Christian.

One night I asked, "Why should we use the Bible as an authority? Aren't there other works that are just as good?"

We discussed its unity (in spite of the most controversial subjects being written about by forty different people—shepherds, kings, an army general, priests, a prime minister, fishermen, a physician, and others—over about 1500 years), its prophecies fulfilled down to the details, its scientifically accurate statements no human alive when it was written could have known, its effect on people who follow it. The more I read about the Bible the more convinced I was that it was supernatural. The more I read *in* it, the more convinced I was that it was God's communication to humans—a trustworthy authority, the standard for spirituality and for day-to-day life.

That made Pastor Riggs's and my discussion all the more exciting. Practically every week after prayer meeting, we talked half the night about the Bible. Week after week, I half-expected Pastor Riggs's answers to fall flat in one area or another, as had the answers of previous ministers. Instead, he led me to the Bible for answers to every question. I left our discussions energized, inspired to search the Scripture more deeply and to live by what I learned.

Both the pamphlets and the pastor based every idea on Bible texts. And when I read the texts in context, they truly taught what the pamphlets or pastor said. I studied about salvation, Jesus' second coming, heaven, the Ten Commandments, the day of worship, health habits.

News About Hell

Health habits? These Christians think health habits are related to religion? I read the pamphlet and the texts in the Bible. When I put it all together, I concluded: The condition of the body affects the condition of the mind. Since God speaks to us through our minds, the condition of our minds affects God's ability to speak to us.

Could my raunchy eating habits and lack of exercise be the reason God hasn't spoken to me for a long time?

I'd been so busy since I'd arrived in Waverly that I hadn't taken time for swimming. I kept my weight within reason just by keeping a close eye on the scales and cutting back on food for a couple days whenever I gained a couple pounds. *Lots easier to lose two pounds than forty,* I'd remind myself.

But about the only exercise I got was running during TV commercials across the street to the convenience store for M & M's, Butterfingers, pecan pie pieces, and Almond Hershey bars. As for the rest of my diet—within half a block of my apartment were quick-stop hamburger, chicken, and ice-cream shops. *When was the last time I ate a vegetable?* I wondered. *Oh, yeah, a week and a half ago at the church potluck . . . unless you count French fries, onion rings, and the itty bit of lettuce and tomato on hamburgers. Would God speak to me again if I changed my health habits?* I wondered. *It'd be worth a try,* I decided.

I kept studying and applying each new thing I learned. The Bible was full of things I'd never realized were there. It was relevant to modern life.

But I began to puzzle over why so many different people got so many different things out of the Bible. "Why," I asked Pastor Riggs one evening after prayer meeting, "are there so many differences in churches?"

Chapter Twenty-three

Why So Many Differences?

"What do you mean?" Pastor Riggs asked.

"There's only one Bible. But there are dozens of different churches, and each one thinks they're the only one that's right. Why? How can a person figure out which church to go to?"

"Good questions, Jay. I used to wonder the same things. In fact, I started searching for God and for truth during my Navy days in Vietnam. When I got back home, I'd read the Bible; then I'd go from church to church and just get more confused. Through trial and error, I discovered five principles of Bible study that simplified my spiritual search. I think they're related to your question."

"What are they?" I asked. I sat down on the landscaping timbers that edged raised flower beds by the main entrance of the church.

The pastor sat on the edge of the flower bed across the sidewalk from me. "First, 'pray for God's guidance before you study God's Word.' The confusion about what the Bible teaches should be a warning. Especially since the devil wants us to *mis*understand God.

As you pray for guidance and study the Bible, God will speak to you through it."

I thought back to New Age instructions about spiritual contact—always pray for protection from evil spirits. "Makes sense," I responded.

Pastor Riggs shifted his weight. "Second, study the Bible with an open mind. Don't go to the Bible to prove what you already think. Let it speak its truth to you."

"Hm-m-m. I can relate to that," I said. "I've always been curious and open-minded. Want to get to the basics of truth. About everything—airplanes, radio, God." I shook my head. "I don't understand people who make up their minds without evidence and refuse to face facts."

Pastor Riggs grinned and nodded.

"Like the adage," I said, "'Some people's minds are like concrete—all mixed up and set.'"

"That's about right with some." He chuckled then turned serious again. "But with spiritual issues, eternity's at stake. It's pretty important to let God speak."

His words hung in the silence, then he continued, "The Bible doesn't always say what you think it's going to. But, over the years, I've discovered that Bible truth is beautiful. I just need to give God the chance to make it clear."

I thought of my early disenchantment with God, then of the things I'd learned later. "I couldn't agree more."

"Another principle," Pastor Riggs said, "is, read passages in context. Whether you read Scripture, the newspaper, or Shakespeare, if you pick a phrase or a section without reading what's around it, you may totally misinterpret it.

He grinned. "Did you hear about the man who thought he

ought to read the Bible for guidance but he didn't know where to start?"

"Don't think so."

"He closed his Bible, then let it fall open." Pastor Riggs demonstrated as he spoke. "Without looking, he raised his hand, then brought his pointing finger down on the open Bible. The verse said: Judas 'went and hanged himself.' 'That's not a good devotional to start my day,' he thought. 'I'll try again.' So he turned a section of pages and pointed again. This time the words at his fingertip said, 'Go and do thou likewise.'"

I shifted on the edge of the flower bed. "I hope the story's fiction."

"Probably," Pastor Riggs admitted, "but some people believe things that are just about as foolish because they don't read whole passages."

I nodded in agreement. "I've seen it happen," I said, thinking back. I laughed. "Maybe the ministers I ran into years ago knew something you don't."

"What's that?"

"All they had to do was use a text out of context and I was gone. I didn't stick around and hound them with questions week after week after week."

Pastor Riggs grinned. His dark eyes sparkled.

"Just think of all the nights you could have gotten home early instead of putting up with all my questions hour after hour."

He laughed. "Just wait till I tell my wife I have a new method for cutting down my work hours."

Neither of us would have laughed so hard had it not been ludicrous to think of Pastor Riggs that way.

"Seriously," he said when we quieted, "always read a text in context. Ask yourself, 'What did the writer mean?' It's so-o-o important! You can make the Bible say some really weird things if you just take parts and pieces."

"I'm certainly with you on that," I said.

"Good. Fourth, 'Read everything the Bible says on a topic.'" He paused as if searching for words. "Don't build a doctrine or philosophy on one or two texts, especially if there are other texts that seem not to agree."

"What do you mean?" I asked. "Can't we depend on every text in the Bible?"

"Absolutely. But there are a few that, if read out of context and taken by themselves, may seem to say one thing when other Scriptures clearly say something different. But I've never found any real contradictions. If I study a little deeper and read everything the Bible says about a topic, the answers become clear."

"But doesn't that take a lot of time?"

He smiled. "Well, yeah, it does take some time. But . . . tell me, if a husband and wife don't spend much time together, what kind of friendship do they have?"

One of my eyebrows lurched upward. I thought of my own three wives, three divorces, too many hours at work, not enough time at home. I sighed. "Little time, little friendship."

"It's the same with God," Pastor Riggs said. "With every hour I spend in the Scriptures, I learn to know God better. Because God is love, the better I get to know Him, the more I love and trust Him."

The words hung in the still spring air. "OK," I finally said. "One, pray for God's guidance." I counted the principles off on my fingers. "Two, keep an open mind. Three, context. Four, read everything on the topic. Didn't you say there were five?"

"You're a good student, Jay. Yes, there are five. The last one is this: Study for yourself. I'm a pastor, and I love to study the Bible with people. But don't take my word for what it says. Don't take anybody's word for truth. You are responsible to God for what you do with truth.

"Study with others; listen to others. That's fine. But, bottom line, study till you know for yourself what God says in the Bible."

Pastor Riggs smiled broadly. He lifted both arms and gestured freely. "God's truth is liberating. God's truth brings the greatest joy possible. Don't let anyone steal God's joy from you. Study till you know God."

I swatted a bug that buzzed to a landing on my arm. "I don't mean to be disrespectful . . . but I don't really see anything earthshaking in that list. I mean . . . that's basically the way I've studied radio programming or management or anything else I wanted to learn. It's . . . just logical."

"You're right, Jay. The principles are simple. But they're extremely important. If you'll follow them, then find a church that agrees with the Bible, you'll do fine."

I scratched my head.

"Unfortunately, Jay," Pastor Riggs continued, "it's really easy to accept certain beliefs, to get comfortable with them, and then to quit searching for truth. Keep following those Bible study principles the rest of your life. Let God change you as He leads you."

"So . . . getting down to the nitty-gritty," I asked skeptically, "are you saying that there really is only one church that has truth and that all true Christians belong to your church?"

"No. I'm saying that every human being ought to investigate truth. We're born babies and grow physically. Even after we reach our full height, till the day we die, new cells grow and replace worn out ones. A person who doesn't grow physically, mentally, or emotionally is severely handicapped. Don't you think we ought to grow spiritually too?"

"Well . . . yes."

"I'm saying," he continued, "that all Christians, whether they're in my church or any other church, ought to continue to study the Bible." He looked off into the distance, as if thinking, then continued. "Friends of God search for, value, and follow truth because it leads them into deeper and fuller friendship with God."

At home that night I prayed, "God, I want to be Your friend. Please help me to understand truth. Please give me the love and joy that comes from being Yours."

At work, every third time I passed Jennifer's desk, she had something more to say about my dating her friend. "No, Jennifer. Forget it. I'm not interested."

"But she's really nice."

"I don't care how nice she is! I'm not interested in dating anyone. Inki and I are doing just fine by ourselves, thank you. And I like it this way!"

Why won't she catch on and leave me alone? I have more than enough stress without a woman on top of it all! In my adult life, I'd never been without a partner for long. Now I realized it had been two years since Keyli and I split. In two years I hadn't gone on a single date. Being alone had been a new experience, but my resolve to stay single forever hadn't weakened an iota.

I looked forward to the weekend. One of the benefits of my job was an occasional all-expenses-paid weekend in Nashville. I ate well, and Inki and I stayed at a nice hotel. My favorite spot was the swimming pool. I'd swim and lounge, lounge and swim. The total relaxation contrasted completely with my regular pace.

Poolside, this trip, I pondered what I'd been learning. Some things had surprised me. Some had been downright shocking. But everything was straight from the Bible. It made sense. It all fit together.

I'd been praying for truth. That was easy when I thought I

knew truth. But I'd learned a lot of new information in the last few months, a lot of corrections to former misunderstandings about God. Only one pamphlet was left—"Are the Dead Really Dead?"

Annette, the pamphlets, Pastor Riggs—they all used Bible texts carefully. The new information I was learning jigsawed together into a nearly-complete, beautiful picture. But they had to be wrong in this last pamphlet. I had studied about life and death for years. I had experienced former lives. I had read what spirits claiming to be advanced souls spoke or wrote through individuals like Edgar Cayce and Ruth Montgomery.

I spent more time in my hotel room than usual—studying the Bible. By the end of the weekend, I was eager to question Pastor Riggs. After prayer meeting, I started in. Again, he led me to Bible answers. Finally I asked, "What if I can prove to you I'm right about what happens when a person dies?"

"Then I'll quit this church and join a New Age church," he responded instantly. "Maybe become a New Age pastor."

"You really would?"

"Absolutely!" he exclaimed without a second's hesitation. "In the last few verses of the Bible, where God is wrapping up what He wants us to know, He gives us two solemn warnings: One, don't add to Scripture, or the plagues will be added to you; and, two, don't take away from Scripture or your name will be taken away from the book of life and from all the joys of heaven [Revelation 22: 18, 19]. Truth is a serious matter. I don't care what it is. If it's truth from God's Word, I want it."

I will show Pastor Riggs the truth about reincarnation! I resolved. *He's such a vibrant Christian now. He'll be dynamite when he understands reincarnation!*

Chapter Twenty-four

Study Time

No better time to start convincing Pastor Riggs than right now, I thought. "Let me ask you this."

"Yes?"

"How can the Bible speak of the immortal soul one moment and the next say we are dead after we die and there is no conscious thought again until we are resurrected?"

"Immortal soul?" Pastor Riggs questioned. "Where does the Bible speak of 'immortal soul'?"

"Well, I don't know, right off. But I believe it does."

Pastor Riggs looked out over the horse pasture next to the church for a long minute. When he turned back, he said, "You know, Jay, I've searched and searched my Bible for that phrase, but I can't find it."

His words shocked me. Never one to back off from a challenge, I headed home to study until I found the phrase "immortal soul" in the Bible. Every evening after work, I read and studied and searched. I found lots of references to 'soul' and one to 'immortal.' But the two words were never together.

"But it *has* to be there!" I told Pastor Riggs after prayer meeting the next week. "Religious leaders say 'immortal soul' all the time. Where did it come from?"

"I don't know," he said, "but certainly not from the Bible."

Nearby, a cricket chorus fiddled.

It's time for me to study in depth, I decided. *Time to debunk the silly theory these Christians believe about what happens when a person dies.*

Pastor Riggs had a faraway look like he was thinking too. Finally he spoke again. "I think death is one of the most misunderstood subjects in the Bible, Jay. To many, it's a mystery. Many fear it. Many believe their loved ones who've died aren't dead at all but live on in some other condition. Most world religions teach that when people die they become spirits. It's important to know what happens when a person dies for a couple reasons: First, living is easier if you don't have to worry about dying. Second, misunderstanding death makes a person vulnerable to being deceived by Satan on other issues."

"Deceived on other issues?" I asked. "How?"

"Have you studied the pamphlet on death?" Pastor Riggs asked.

"Not yet."

"It will be easier to answer that question satisfactorily if you understand what happens at death," he said. "How about if you study that and then we discuss any questions you have?"

As soon as I arrived home, I curled into the love seat. "God," I prayed, "I do want to know truth. Please lead me as I study and protect me from evil spirits." I opened the pamphlet, "Are the Dead Really Dead?"

"How did we get here in the first place? 'And the Lord God

formed man of the dust of the ground, and breathed into his nostrils the breath of life; and man became a living soul.' Genesis 2:7."

Interesting. Essentially, a body of dust plus breath equals a living soul. I found the verse in my own Bible, read the context, and concluded, *"A living soul is a living person."*

I turned back to the pamphlet: "What happens when a person dies? 'Then shall the dust return to the earth as it was: and the spirit shall return unto God who gave it' (Ecclesiastes 12:7)."

What?

I looked back to the text, then looked it up in my Bible and read it in context. *It doesn't delineate between the righteous and the wicked. The spirit of everyone who dies returns to God? That's surely not what I learned in church. I learned there was a big difference where the spirit went—the difference between heaven and hell.*

But that's right, I thought. *It fits with reincarnation. All people— good or bad—go on to a spiritual plane where they can evaluate their past life and then go on to another.*

The booklet went on to ask what the spirit was and quoted two texts. I looked them up in my own Bible—the Bible my parents had given me when I was twelve. James 2:26 read, "For as the body without the spirit is dead . . ." The note about "spirit" in the margin said: "Or, breath." Job 27:3 said, "All the while my breath is in me, and the spirit of God is in my nostrils." About "spirit," the marginal reference said, "That is, the breath which God gave him."

Breath is what's in our nostrils. And certainly, the body without breath is dead. But isn't the spirit more than that? Aren't the spirit and the soul the same?

But just a minute. They can't be the same . . . if the Bible is right. That verse in Genesis said a body (or dust) plus spirit (or breath) is a living soul (or a living being).

So what happens when the breath or spirit goes back to God?

Falling for a Lie

Psalm 104:29: "Thou [God] takest away their breath, they die, and return to their dust."

Essentially, there are two equations:

Dust + breath = soul.

Soul - breath = dust.

But just a minute. Isn't it the soul that lives on from one life to another?

"The soul that sinneth, it shall die" (Ezekiel 18:20). Job 4:17 spoke of "mortal man." My dictionary defined *mortal* as "subject to death." First Timothy 6:16 described God as "who only hath immortality."

So . . . according to the Bible, only God has unending existence? But that can't be. I'm misunderstanding something. I know better than that . . . through my early Christian training AND through New Age.

My head was swimming. I glanced at my watch. *Oh-oh. If I don't get to bed soon, I'll be worthless tomorrow.* Reluctantly, I laid study materials aside.

Thoughts of body, soul, and spirit intruded into my dreams that night.

Work the next day was busy as usual. That night when I got home from work, I eagerly resumed studying about death.

I reviewed what I'd read the night before, then went on. "Do good people go to heaven when they die?" the booklet asked.

"'All that are in the graves shall hear his voice, and shall come forth' (John 5:28, 29). 'David . . . is both dead and buried, and his sepulchre is with us unto this day. For David is not ascended into the heavens' (Acts 2:29, 34)."

Hm-m-m. People don't go either to heaven or hell when they die? They wait in their graves for resurrection day? This was new to me. But what do the dead do? What do they know?

"'The living know that they shall die: but the dead know not any thing, neither have they any more a reward; for the memory of them is forgotten. Also their love, and their hatred, and their envy, is now perished; neither have they any more a portion for ever in any thing that is done under the sun. . . . there is no work, nor device, nor knowledge, nor wisdom in the grave, whither thou goest' (Ecclesiastes 9:5, 6, 10). 'The dead praise not the Lord' (Psalm 115:17)."

That doesn't leave much. The dead know nothing. They have no memory, no love, no hate, no envy. No emotion. They don't work. They don't even praise God.

I pondered what I was reading. *According to these Bible texts, people who die don't become angels or spirits. They can't bring us messages.* I scowled. *I've seen spirits. I've heard messages from them. Something's fishy.*

Hm-m-m, I wondered, *did Jesus say anything about death when He was here?* I'd barely questioned when I remembered *He raised his friend Lazarus from death.*

I found the story in John 11. In verses 11-14, Jesus talked specifically about Lazarus' death: "Our friend Lazarus sleepeth; but I go, that I may awake him out of sleep. Then said his disciples, Lord, if he sleep, he shall do well. Howbeit Jesus spake of his death: but they thought that he had spoken of taking of rest in sleep. Then said Jesus unto them plainly, Lazarus is dead."

Sleep. Interesting word to describe death. In sleep you're "dead" to the world. You know nothing, do nothing. So how long do the dead sleep?

"'So man lieth down, and riseth not: till the heavens be no more' (Job 14:12). 'The day of the Lord will come . . . in the which the heavens shall pass away' (2 Peter 3:10)."

"What happens to the righteous dead at the second coming of

Falling for a Lie

Christ?" At "the day of the Lord"?

"'Behold, I come quickly; and my reward is with me, to give every man according as his work shall be' (Revelation 22:12). 'The Lord himself shall descend from heaven with a shout, . . . and the dead in Christ shall rise . . . and so shall we ever be with the Lord' (1 Thessalonians 4:16, 17). 'We shall all be changed, In a moment, in the twinkling of an eye, . . . and the dead shall be raised incorruptible. . . . For this corruptible must put on incorruption, and this mortal must put on immortality' (1 Corinthians 15:51-53)."

These texts clearly taught that when a person dies they simply cease to live. They sleep in their grave until Jesus comes at the end of the world and resurrects them. In earlier study I had learned that people do not go to either heaven or hell until after they are resurrected. God's followers then go to heaven for eternal life and those who reject God go to hell where they are destroyed.

But this simply can't be right. I will use the Bible study principle Pastor Riggs recommended—read every text about a topic.

Through the week I studied and restudied all the verses I could find about death. I searched for other texts. Finally, I discovered a few that conflicted with what this pamphlet taught! Was I ever relieved. By prayer meeting evening, I was ready to convert the pastor to New Age.

Chapter Twenty-five

Converting the Pastor

"I think I understand what the pamphlet on death said," I told Pastor Riggs after the next prayer meeting.

"Good. What do you understand the Bible to say about what happens when a person dies?"

"According to the pamphlet," I hedged, "when a person dies they simply cease to exist. Their breath goes back to God and their body goes to the grave. When Jesus returns to earth, everyone who has died will be resurrected. Those who accepted Jesus will go to heaven. Those who didn't will be destroyed in hell."

"So, what do you think of that?" Pastor Riggs asked.

"Well, it's surely different than I grew up thinking. And it's different than what I learned later. I still have some questions."

"Great!" he shot back. "I love it when people think! When they really study things out and think them through." He sat down on the edge of one of the raised flower beds like he was settling in for another long night. "What's on your mind?"

Falling for a Lie

Even though I should have expected it, I still marveled that anyone would listen to all my questions. And not only listen—Pastor Riggs treated me as though he respected me, as though he thought I was asking intelligent questions. Even after he'd dealt with them by the hour, week after week.

"One of the Bible study principles you suggested was to read everything on a topic. So I did some more reading."

"Good. What did you find?"

"What about the thief on the cross—the one Jesus forgave? Didn't Jesus say he'd go to paradise that day?"

"Let's look at the story," Pastor Riggs said, opening his Bible. Turning pages whispered into the evening only a moment before he said, "Here it is—Luke 23."

We read the story together, then Pastor Riggs said, "Let's read another account about Jesus' time on the cross. And then let's keep reading until after His resurrection. It's in John, chapters 19 and 20."

We read through Jesus' crucifixion, death, burial, resurrection, and His talking with Mary in the garden.

"So on Sunday morning after Jesus' resurrection, when he talked with Mary, had he been to see His Father in heaven yet?"

I looked back down at the verses we'd just read. "In John 20:17 Jesus said, 'I am not yet ascended to my Father.' So he must not have gone to heaven until after that on Sunday morning."

"Right. So, is there a contradiction? Luke 23:43 says Jesus told the thief on Friday, 'Today you'll be with me in paradise.' But on Sunday morning He told Mary He hadn't been to paradise yet."

"Sounds like a contradiction."

"It looks like it on the surface," he responded, "but let's look a little deeper. As originally written, the Greek had no punctuation. Periods, commas, semicolons—none of them were there. The punctuation as we see it in our Bibles today was put in by translators. I'm grateful for what they did, but I think once in a while they goofed.

"Let's look at verse 43 again," he continued. "What if the comma came after 'today' instead of before it?"

"'Verily I say unto you today,'" I read, "'thou shalt be with me in paradise.'" I drummed the eraser of my pencil on my open Bible. "That says 'I'm talking to you today' rather than 'I'll be with you today.' "

"Also," Pastor Riggs added, "in the Greek, grammatically, the 'today' could go with either the phrase before or the phrase after. I believe in Jesus' words in Luke 23:43 just as I believe in the rest of the Bible. But since the rest of the Bible indicates a person is unconscious in death, since Jesus Himself called death a sleep and said He hadn't been to paradise yet since He died, since grammatically 'today' could go with either phrase, and since the punctuation in our Bibles is not inspired, moving the comma makes sense to me. Otherwise, this text would conflict with many."

Page 177

"True," I said. "Even Jesus would conflict with Himself."

"Right," Pastor Riggs agreed. "Does that make sense?"

"Yes," I said thoughtfully, "it does." A light breeze rustled Bible pages. "Either the Bible agrees with itself or it doesn't. And if it doesn't, then we ought to throw it out."

"You're right, Jay."

"Well, then, I need to get the rest of my questions answered so I can know for myself whether or not the Bible is worth following."

"And your next question is?"

"What about Matthew 10:28 where Jesus said, 'Fear not them which kill the body, but are not able to kill the soul?'" I asked. "Sounds to me like the soul lives on beyond the body. Doesn't that support reincarnation?"

Falling for a Lie

"Let's look at it."

I was used to hearing that phrase. It was one of the reasons I respected Pastor Riggs. He didn't spout off his opinion or some philosophical answer. We looked at our Bibles together and read and studied until the answers came clear.

We each found the text. Pastor Riggs scanned nearby verses as he often did. "Jesus is preparing His disciples for persecution here. Why don't you read all of verse 28?"

"'And fear not them which kill the body, but are not able to kill the soul: but rather fear him which is able to destroy both soul and body in hell.'"

"Actually, what's the last part of the verse say about the soul?" Pastor Riggs asked.

"It can be destroyed." I scratched my head. "How'd I miss that when I was studying at home?"

"So, now that you're reading the whole thing, what does that verse say?"

I read it again. Then I read several verses before and after it. "Essentially, Jesus is saying, 'Don't let people persecuting you scare you. Even if they kill you, it's not really a big deal. Because you'll be raised in the resurrection. And they won't be able to do a thing about it. What you should fear is living so that you'll suffer the second death. There's no resurrection from that.'"

"Great paraphrase."

I shook my head. "I can't believe I missed the last half of that verse. I've discredited ministers because they didn't use texts accurately. Because they didn't consider context. I just did the same thing."

A frog croaked nearby. "From what I see," Pastor Riggs said, "you appear to be a sincere seeker. You want to know truth. Right?"

"Yes. Definitely."

"Is it true that it would be easier for you to believe in reincarnation than to believe that people are unconscious in death?"

"Absolutely."

"I don't question your sincerity at all, Jay. But maybe this is a good example. When we read the Bible it's so-o-o easy to see what we want to see . . ."

"Instead of what it really says," I added. "I'm going to have to keep practicing those Bible study principles you shared. Several of them apply to this situation. Pray for God's guiding, an open mind, context, and read everything the Bible says on the topic. That's four out of five."

"The fifth one applies too," Pastor Riggs added. "Don't just take my word for it. When you go home, study it out for yourself."

"I will."

"You must study for yourself," Pastor Riggs said, "but this points to one of the reasons it's good to study the Bible with others too. They may have seen something we missed. Or we may have an insight they didn't see. When people who want truth study together, they each grow."

"Like the Bible study class," I observed. "Everyone studies the same Bible text at home then discusses them. I'm amazed at the different insights of various people."

"That's one of the reasons Jesus established the 'church' idea. We get to know Him better by fellowshiping and studying together."

"I can see that."

I continued throwing questions at Pastor Riggs. With each, we looked at Scriptures, and there were good and reasonable explanations. I was down to the last text I'd found that contradicted the death-is-sleep theory. But it was a good one to support reincarnation.

"How about 1 Peter 4:6? Doesn't it say the gospel was preached to dead people?"

He turned Bible pages then scanned. "Go ahead and read verse 6."

"'For this cause was the gospel preached also to them that are dead, that they might be judged according to men in the flesh, but live according to God in the spirit.'"

"'For this cause was. . .'" Pastor Riggs said. "What tense of verb is 'was'?"

"Past."

"Right. 'For this cause *was* the gospel preached also to them that are dead.' What tense is 'are'?"

"Present."

"So," he concluded, "the gospel *was* preached, while they were living, to those who *are* dead now."

I reread the text. "Hm-m-m."

"This is an interesting text," Pastor Riggs continued. "May I give you a really loose paraphrase?"

"Sure."

"Verse 4—Your old cronies think it really strange that you don't run riot with them like you used to. Verse 5—But they're going to face judgment too. Both the living and dead will face judgment. Verse 6—But don't worry about your friends who are already dead. Yes, they'll face judgment too. But God sent people to preach to them while they were still alive."

I looked back through the verses. His paraphrase didn't do it injustice.

"In other words," he continued, "God is absolutely fair. He's not going to require of you in the judgment something that you didn't have the opportunity to know about. That sounds to me like *good* news!"

"You're right," I agreed. "That's wonderful news."

"The devil's trying to make God out to be an ogre. Too many

people believe that. But God is kind. God is wonderful. God is patient beyond any patience we can comprehend. God is love."

Lights had glowed from the homes near us for some time. Crickets cr-r-ricked, and a frog with a bass voice croaked repeatedly into the night.

"I guess that's why I keep coming back." I sighed and shifted on the edge of the flower bed across from Pastor Riggs. "Every Christian church I've ever been in before said 'God is love,' but their doctrines denied it. Hell, for instance. A God who tortures people for hundreds and millions of years . . . that's worse than Hitler!" I shuddered. "How could heaven be happy if someone you loved was frying and crying in hell?" I asked into the night, not expecting an answer. "I see the sense in what you teach."

Only nature's night sounds broke the silence for an eternity. Then I spoke again. "But I've given reincarnation twenty years of my life. My whole life was based on it. They told me the Bible and reincarnation agreed with each other. Was I wrong all this time?"

"What I teach," Pastor Riggs said, "isn't important unless . . ."

I picked up his words. "Unless it's from the Bible. . . . And it has been. Everything. Everything's been straight out of the Bible." My heart was in my throat. "But we're missing something some-place. Like . . . well . . . the dead communicating with us. I know they do. I've heard them. I've seen a spirit with my own eyes. I've seen visions of things that no human being could know. I know it was real!"

"I don't question that it was real," Pastor Riggs said.

I held up my Bible. "If this is right," I challenged, "how can the dead communicate with us?"

Chapter Twenty-six

"How Can the Dead Communicate With Us?"

"How can the dead communicate with us?" Pastor Riggs repeated as he looked off into the night sky studded with stars.

After a long minute, he looked back at me. "That's another really good question, Jay. Maybe the best way to look at it is to go right back to the first mention of death in Scripture." He turned back practically to the front cover of his Bible. "God warned about death right away in Genesis 2 so we could avoid it." He ran his finger down the page.

I turned to Genesis 2 in my Bible also.

Pastor Riggs looked up. "God gave Adam and Eve a luxurious estate to live in. But, remember our earlier discussion about Satan?"

"Yeah."

"Again, in a nutshell, long before Adam and Eve, Satan accused God of being a tyrant. Accused Him of not allowing freedom. Then Satan started campaigning among the hosts of angels God had created.

"God knew Satan was wrong. But God is ultimately fair. He doesn't force. He allowed the angels to look at the evidence and make their own choice. That was the price of freedom."

God doesn't force. That thought hit home with me. *God respects our freedom. In a small way,* I thought, *like I respected Keyli's. It cost me. But it was the right thing to do.*

"Eventually," Pastor Riggs continued, "two-thirds of the angels were loyal to God. But a third of heaven's angels chose to believe Satan. So sin and suffering would not live on and on forever, God exiled Satan from heaven.

"When God created Adam and Eve, Satan wanted to alienate them from God too. To get them to honor him. But God wouldn't allow Satan free reign to tempt them with his lies. Satan could only come to one single tree to try to convince humans that his way was better than God's. Adam and Eve could happily eat from any of the plants and bushes and trees all over that estate except for that one. And God warned them to stay away from that one to avoid death. Well, here, why don't you read verse 17."

"'But of the tree of the knowledge of good and evil, thou shalt not eat of it: for in the day that thou eatest thereof thou shalt surely die,' " I read.

"So what happened?" Pastor Riggs went on. "We don't know whether it was three days, a couple years, or a century, but a few verses later Eve is standing at the one tree she was warned to avoid. And there she is, talking to a snake in that tree. In chapter 3, verse 1, the snake says, 'Hath God said, Ye shall not eat of every tree of the garden?' Eve says they can eat from all but one. And the serpent responds in verses 4 and 5: 'Ye shall not surely die: For God doth know that in the day ye eat thereof, then your eyes shall be opened, and ye shall be as gods, knowing good and evil.'

"God said, 'You'll die if you eat of that tree.' The serpent said,

Falling for a Lie

'You won't die. Furthermore, you can't trust God.' But just a minute. Who was the serpent?"

Remembering back to the earlier study, I replied, "Satan . . . in disguise, of course."

"And what is Satan's purpose for humans?"

"He's trying to get us to go along with him. Trying to hurt God by destroying the people God loves."

"Exactly. And how does he do that?"

"He deceives."

Page 184

"Right. Take a look at John 8:44."

We each found it. When I first started studying with Pastor Riggs, it took me forever to find texts in the Bible. But I'd gotten well acquainted with Scripture over the last few months. I found John 8 nearly as quickly as he.

"Jesus is speaking here. What does He say about the devil?" he asked.

I looked at the context then read through the verse. "That he was 'a murderer from the beginning,' had 'no truth in him,' and 'he is a liar, and the father of it.'"

"So," Pastor Riggs continued, "God said, 'You'll die if you eat of that tree.' Satan said, 'You won't die.' Would you agree that the two statements conflict?"

"Definitely."

"And the two who made the statements were God and the devil and, according to Jesus, the devil is a liar?"

"Right."

"So who should Eve believe?"

"God, of course."

"So, would you say what the devil said was a lie?"

"Yes."

"There's something else interesting about this encounter. When was the last time you visited with a snake?"

"Can't say I ever have."

"Nor me. Snakes don't talk. Right?"

"Right."

"But the snake in the Garden of Eden did. Satan spoke through the medium of a snake."

It all started coming together in my mind. "Wow! I think I'm getting the picture." I swallowed hard. "Millions believe Satan's lie—that we don't die. Eastern religions, New Age, even a lot of Christians. They say we live on immediately after death, in one form or another."

"You hit the nail on the head," Pastor Riggs responded. "Many people think that if something is supernatural, it has to be from God. But Jesus talked about that. Look at Mark 13:22. Jesus is talking there about what will happen as it gets close to the time when He will come back to this earth."

"'For false Christs and false prophets shall rise, and shall shew signs and wonders, to seduce, if it were possible, even the elect,'" I read.

"Later," Pastor Riggs said, "Paul talked about the same thing. Look at 2 Thessalonians 2:9 and 10. What kinds of things does Satan do?"

"Interesting. Satan works with 'power and signs and lying wonders, and with all deceivableness of unrighteousness.'"

"Satan can do some miracles," Pastor Riggs said, "and speaking through mediums is one of his miracles."

My eyes popped open wider. My eyebrows raised. "Great. God does miracles and Satan does miracles. How do I know which is which?"

"You're getting to the crux of the matter, Jay. John addressed that in one of his letters to the early church—in 1 John." He turned pages. "Here. Chapter 4. Look at verse 1—'Beloved, believe not every spirit, but try the spirits whether they are of God: because many false prophets are gone out into the world.' But he doesn't stop there. Verse 2—'Hereby know ye the Spirit of God:' In other words, here's how to know. Read verses 2 and 3."

"'Hereby know ye the Spirit of God: Every spirit that confesseth that Jesus Christ is come in the flesh is of God: And every spirit that confesseth not that Jesus Christ is come in the flesh is not of God: and this is that spirit of antichrist . . .'" I read parts of the text silently again. "So, what's it mean to confess that Jesus Christ came in the flesh?"

"Jesus claimed to be God," Pastor Riggs said. "He claimed to fulfill the prophecies that God would become human and pay the price for all humans so they could be reunited with God. In John's day, some began saying Jesus was a good man but not God. Some said He was God but He wasn't really human. Various theories spread. But John says, if a teacher doesn't accept Jesus for who Scripture says He is, that teacher is not from God. Doesn't matter what else they say. Doesn't matter if they perform miracles. Doesn't matter if they tell you things you thought nobody else knew. Doesn't matter if things they tell you about the future happen. If they say Jesus is other than what Scripture says He is, they have a spirit other than God's." Pastor Riggs let silence hang then broke it with, "Have you heard that Jesus was just a good man? A great teacher, but not God?"

"I certainly have!"

"Have you heard that Jesus is one of many gods?"

"Yes!"

"Have you heard that humans can become gods?"

"Yes." A thought surprised me. "Hey! That was one of Satan's lies in the Garden of Eden, wasn't it? 'Ye shall be as gods.'"

"That's right, Jay. And Satan's deceiving a lot of people with it."

I shook my head, pondering the lies I'd believed.

Pastor Riggs added another question. "Have you heard that you can work your way to higher planes by your own actions?"

"Yes! And I've told a lot of others."

"When the angel announced Jesus' birth to Joseph, he said, 'Thou shalt call his name Jesus: for he shall save his people from their sins' (Matthew 1:21). And, why don't you read what Peter said in Acts 4:12?"

While I was finding the text, he explained, "Peter and John were arrested for preaching about Jesus. The words in Acts 4:12 are part of Peter's comments to the very people who had them arrested."

"'Neither is there salvation in any other:'" I read, "'for there is none other name under heaven given among men, whereby we must be saved.'"

"Isaiah," Pastor Riggs said, "says ALL our righteousness is as filthy rags—bloody, putrid, stinking rags [Isaiah 64:6]. Not just one or two good things we do are worthless. *All* our righteousness. Every good thing you have ever done in all your life, every good thing I've done since I was born, when we list them *all*, it's like a stack of dirty, stinking rags.

"I can't save myself from Satan's control," Pastor Riggs continued. "The human race, through Adam and Eve, gave control over to Satan. And Satan's a deceiver. He's smarter than I am. I will forever be under Satan's control *until* I accept Jesus for who He is— God who became human so He can be my Saviour.

"Do you see why Satan wants you to believe Jesus isn't everything the Bible says He is?"

"Yeah." I sighed. "If I don't choose to accept Jesus as Saviour, I'm going along with the devil."

Falling for a Lie

Pastor Riggs let that sink in. Finally, he broke the silence. "Let's look at a couple more verses—start with Isaiah 8:19."

I turned to it and read—"'And when they shall say unto you, Seek unto them that have familiar spirits, and unto wizards that peep, and that mutter . . .'" I looked up at Pastor Riggs. "Familiar spirits, wizards—aren't those people who communicate with the dead? People who get communication from someplace other than this world?"

"Right."

I went on reading. "'Should not a people seek unto their God? for the living to the dead?'"

"Why would the living ask questions of the dead? Shouldn't we seek God for answers?" Pastor Riggs paused.

"What about King Saul?" I asked. "When he wanted to talk to the dead prophet Samuel?"

We read the story in 1 Samuel 28. "Notice verse 6," Pastor Riggs said. "The story starts out saying the Lord doesn't answer Saul anymore. So whatever happened, it wasn't from the Lord."

"It was a séance," I concluded. The story reminded me of the voices I heard in a dark basement.

We turned back to Isaiah 8. "Go ahead and read verse 20," Pastor Riggs said.

"'To the law and to the testimony: if they speak not according to this word, it is because there is no light in them.'"

"How do you interpret that?" he asked.

"Well," I said, "looks to me like it's saying the same thing as the verses in 1 John. Look to God for answers. Don't go searching for answers among those He's told you will deceive you. In a sense, it's saying . . . the Bible is the standard."

"Exactly. Solomon said, 'There is a way that seemeth right unto a man, but the end thereof are the ways of death' (Proverbs

16:25). Just because something *seems* right, doesn't mean it is."

Silence weighed heavy. Finally my words poured over despair. "Do you realize what you're telling me?"

"I realize what I'm saying. What are you hearing?"

"Th-th-that . . ." The words were too heavy to enunciate. The night seemed to close in around me. I breathed deeply and sighed several times, trying to relax. "Th-th-that in my search for truth, I found deception?"

Not even a breeze whispered into the long silence.

"I thought I was serving God. More than twenty years." I shook my head and sighed deeply. "Are you telling me I've been serving the devil?"

Chapter Twenty-seven

What Is Truth?

The question echoed through my mind with a dull empty sound—*Are you telling me I've been serving the devil?* But each time the words replayed, they tore at me like a leopard tearing the flesh of fresh kill.

Kind eyes met mine. Softly, Pastor Riggs asked, "Is it *me* that's been telling you anything?"

I sighed again. "No. No, it's not you. It's the Bible." I stood up abruptly and paced back and forth in front of the flower beds. "It's not you. Most of it I've studied at home by myself." I continued pacing . . . back and forth . . . back and forth. "I don't know," I said more to myself than to Pastor Riggs. "I just don't know."

After a long silence, Pastor Riggs said, "Learning more truth isn't always easy. I know. I struggled too. Man, did I struggle."

I stopped at the corner of the flower bed. "What difference does it make what I believe?"

Pastor Riggs inhaled deeply. "Christianity is not just a system of beliefs. It's a personal friendship with God." He looked out over the pasture next door. "Beliefs are like a foundation. If you're building a skyscraper and the foundation is tipped slightly, by the time you get to the fortieth floor, you have a major problem." He paused. "The problem with believing wrongly about God and basic truth is that it distorts the character of God."

A battle raged in my mind. "But . . . does it really matter?"

"I think it does. At the basis, every true doctrine shows that God is love. False beliefs tempt us to think that God is not loving. If we believe that, we end up choosing Satan's principles. And when we live by Satan's principles, we share his unhappiness and, in the end, we'll share his death."

"I just don't know." I groaned. "It'd change everything!"

"Uh-huh."

"Besides, if I've been serving the devil practically my whole adult life, God probably wouldn't even want me."

After another long silence, Pastor Riggs said, "There's a text we've talked about before—1 John 1:9: 'If we confess our sins, he is faithful and just to forgive us our sins, and to cleanse us from all unrighteousness' except stealing cars."

"No, it doesn't say that."

"All unrighteousness except murder?"

"No."

"All unrighteousness except following all the truth you knew?"

"No. There's no 'except.'"

"You're so right, Jay. 'All' covers everything . . . including whatever you've done in the last twenty years."

"I don't know. I just don't know." I glanced at my watch. "It's nearly midnight. I've got to go."

The ride home was a frustrating mental review of the evening. Next day, I worked longer than needed—as long as I concentrated

Falling for a Lie

on work I didn't think about issues of eternity . . . at least not much. That evening news, sitcom, movie—nothing—kept my mind from the Bible.

"OK, OK," I finally groused. I clicked off the TV and grabbed Bible and study materials. I had to be overlooking something! I would find it!

Each evening I delved into my Bible. Even if I forgot about reincarnation, could so many Bible-believing Christians misunderstand what happens when a person dies? I prayed before I studied, as I studied, and at odd hours when thoughts of the subject interrupted sleep or work. I read entire chapters in the Bible, sometimes several chapters, around the texts listed in the study guide. I compared text with text. I scanned whole books of the Bible.

One evening the thought came again that Jesus, while human, was our example in everything. And what happened to Him? He lived, He died, He was buried, He was resurrected. He didn't go to heaven between His death and resurrection. He told Mary He hadn't.

After Lazarus died—when Jesus told Martha, "Thy brother shall rise again," Martha responded, "I know that he shall rise again in the resurrection at the last day." [John 11:23, 24] She didn't say she'd meet him in heaven when she died. She fully believed in resurrection at the end of the world.

It had been easy to say I wanted truth when I agreed with what I learned. It hadn't been bad when I'd learned a few things where I needed to make slight adjustments. But now? When what I was learning was 180 degrees from the bedrock of my belief system?

One day while I was training a new salesperson, she spoke about her involvement with a psychic. As she spoke, I saw warning flags. Bits and pieces of my studying fit together. "You do know, don't you, that messages can come from either good or evil sources?"

"Hey, they work. Doesn't that prove they're OK?"

"No. The devil can give predictions and then make some things happen," I answered. "And when it's him, the end results aren't good."

"I don't care where they come from."

"But the devil doesn't care about you as a person," I persisted. "He wants to hurt God. He wants to cause you misery. He'll do good things for a while to get you hooked, then he'll turn on you."

"What makes you think that?"

"Well, for one thing, I used to use a pendulum. When I first started, it worked for me every time. Answer any question I'd ask it. After I started depending on it, though, it started telling me 'I don't know' or 'I won't tell you' most of the time. I also learned it would lie if its intelligence didn't think the person could handle the truth. That's the problem with the devil. You think he's on your side but, come to find out, he's a plant from the other team, working against you."

She waved me to silence. "Save your breath."

"Would you do just one thing?" I asked.

"What's that?"

"Remember what I've said. You may need it someday."

She snickered. "Oh, yeah. Sure."

I couldn't believe her reaction. During the hour-long drive home that evening, I pondered our discussion and the things I'd been studying. When I walked in my living room, my eyes were drawn to the bookcase. I sensed a question: "What is the source of your books?"

The New Age books. They're NOT from God.

"Do you want something in your home that will deceive you?"

My mind went numb. My heart pounded in my chest. I struggled to breathe. Those books had shaped my thinking through the last twenty-plus years. They had guided my decisions. They had determined the way I lived. They had been a part of the way I treated people. They had helped me find friends. They were my friends.

Those books reminded me of the spiritual fellowship with the study group in Selma. They brought back all the love and respect I felt for Edgar Cayce. They drew me back to my friendship with Hugh Lynn Cayce and Gladys Davis.

"But do you want something in your home that will deceive you?"

A heavy weight settled over me. I clenched my fists and shook my head. "I can't throw them out! I can't do it!"

I picked up one foot like a huge, lead weight. Then the other foot. The twelve feet to the bookcase seemed like three miles.

I raised my hand to the highest shelf, plucked out a New Age book, turned it around, and slid it back into place with its spine facing backwards. One by one I turned each New Age book around. When I had finished, about three-fourths of the books in the book-case showed bared page edges rather than the spines of book covers.

That night I prayed and tried to fit what I was learning about death, hell, resurrection, and Jesus' second coming together into one big picture.

When a person dies, they go to sleep. Their breath returns to God. Their body goes to the grave. They cease to exist. They receive new life when everyone is resurrected, as Jesus was.

After the final judgment, everyone, including those who have followed Satan's deceptions, will acknowledge that God's ways are right.

Satan and his followers will be destroyed in hell's fire. But even that shows love. Those who have chosen Satan's selfish ways would be miserable in a place where all is love and peace. But God does not torture sinners. Hell's fire burns hot and fast. So hot that sinners are burned up. Essentially, they're cremated. Their ashes have no thoughts, no feelings. The person simply ceases to exist.

The people in heaven will cry—they'll miss those who chose not to accept God's gift of salvation. But God will wipe their tears away. Then they'll live joyfully with God and each other throughout eternity.

Sin and suffering will never happen again. Everyone spending eternity with God will know that sin causes pain and suffering. They'll remember, every time they see the scars in Jesus' hands, that sin cost God His life. They'll remember that separating oneself from God brings death. They'll know that God's ways bring peace and joy, freedom and life.

Slowly I realized that what God said in the Bible made even more sense than reincarnation. But I'd grown to love and respect the patient and loving god of reincarnation. How could I turn my back on him?

I longed for the ease of the philosophy of reincarnation that said time waited for me. That no choices would keep me away from God. That bad choices would just mean it would take more lifetimes to get to the heavenly plane. I could make my decision to follow God now or many lifetimes from now.

But the Bible didn't teach that. The Bible said I chose my destiny in one life.

"So why should I accept the Bible rather than New Age books?" I asked aloud. But I knew the answer before I finished the question. I'd been through that earlier. The Bible was clear, had proved itself over centuries, did not contradict itself. I'd been through the arguments for and against it. I knew it was God's Word.

I thought again about what I'd heard a television evangelist say years before. "A Christian minister and a New Age advocate were discussing their destiny. Finally, the New Age advocate asked, 'So, what if I'm right and you're wrong?' 'That wouldn't be a problem for me,' the Christian minister said. 'If reincarnation is right, I'll figure that out after I die and change my beliefs.' After a pause, he asked, 'But what happens if *I* am right?'"

Now, I whispered the answer, "It's the end. There is no second chance."

Suddenly a thought struck me with power. I heard no voice. I just knew with certainty, "What you have been studying is truth."

A sinking feeling washed over me. My head pounded. My hands turned cold and clammy.

"Try the spirits!" my mind quoted from the Bible. *I won't listen to voices, to impressions, to anything unless it agrees with Scripture!*

My heart raced.

"It does agree with Scripture," I whispered. "I've studied it. I've searched the whole Bible. When I put every Bible text and every Bible story together, there's no question. Death is a sleep. The alarm clock doesn't ring till the resurrection at the end of the world."

Shivering I stood, then paced the living room. I glanced at the backwards New Age books on the shelf as I paced by. I got a drink of water, washed dishes, and paced some more. I marched to the convenience store for fruit juice, then returned to wear a deeper track in the living room carpet.

"It is truth!" I finally shouted toward the ceiling. Then I collapsed into the love seat. "What am I going to do with it?"

Chapter Twenty-eight

Wrestling Peace

I wrestled with the decision for weeks. *It is truth. What am I going to do with it?*

I prayed for the light of God's guidance. I read the Bible. I searched the pamphlets for errors. I read the Bible more—whole sections, whole books. *What's the WHOLE picture?* I asked over and over again.

From time to time Annette suggested places in the Bible to look for texts that talked about life and death. One day when frustration was boiling inside me, I asked her if she could stop by my apartment after work and answer some questions for me.

She squinted, like she was checking her mental calendar. "Sure. Tonight I could stop by. I don't know if I can answer your questions, but I can always say 'I don't know,' and we can look together for the answer, or I can go home and study the Bible till I find it."

Annette arrived at my door that evening, her peaceful, relaxed self. Within minutes her face had changed—calmness had disappeared, taut lines pulled at her cheeks. It was almost like I'd seen the Tennessee hills change when golden sunlight disappeared and charcoal thunderclouds rolled in.

"Jay," she gasped, "I've got to get out of here." She stood and headed for the door. Her face was flushed. She coughed. She wheezed. She choked out the words, "I can't breathe!"

Puzzled, I followed her outside. "What's wrong? Can I help?"

"Let's walk," she said.

At least she was breathing now.

I made sure the door was closed so Inki couldn't follow us. We headed up the middle of the little-used side street in silence.

We'd walked about a quarter of a block when I noticed a puppy ahead on the sidewalk bouncing around on its leash. It had grown beyond the cute cuddly stage, into the awkward, gangly, big-feet stage. Then the puppy looked our direction. Immediately, it yelped and started barking. But its bark was no puppy yip. It was a repeated wail of terror.

The middle-aged man holding the dog's leash looked around at us then back at the puppy. "It's all right, Mack. It's all right. Come."

The puppy didn't come. He stared our direction. He strained backwards on his leash, keeping as far away from us as possible. He howled. He growled.

We kept walking toward the dog and his owner, but in the middle of the street.

The puppy took a couple halting steps toward us, as if he thought he ought to attack. Then he shrank back, his tail between his legs.

"Easy, Mack," the owner comforted. "Come," he ordered again.

Mack didn't come. His eyes were riveted toward Annette and me. His hackles raised.

As we neared, I noticed Mack was not looking at me. I glanced over at Annette, then back at the puppy. He was not looking at Annette either. He was looking around us—above us and on either side.

Mack's owner walked toward him, shortening the leash as he went. He knelt beside the dog and pulled him close. "It's OK, Mack. Quiet." He patted the dog. "It's OK."

Mack kept barking, growling, and howling. His eyes kept darting *around* Annette and me.

The owner looked up as we passed. He looked totally baffled. "I'm sorry." He shook his head. "I don't know what got into him. He's never done this before."

I shrugged. "It's OK."

"I take him walking every night," he continued. "We've met up with all kinds of people. With animals, skateboards, bicycles, motorcycles. He's never acted like this. I don't know what's wrong with him."

In my days in the occult, I'd experienced terror when I saw a spirit. I'd read that animals sometimes see into a dimension that humans can't. That they can see spirits—either good or bad ones. I was convinced the puppy saw something no one else saw. Given the terror he exhibited, what he saw had to be evil.

The commotion stopped after we'd passed.

"Any idea what was going on?" I asked Annette.

"I don't know . . . but it's weird," she responded. "From the moment . . . I entered . . . your apartment . . . I felt a chill. A dark . . . heavy presence. I heard voices. I felt . . . like someone was going to stab me . . . in the back. Like a vice . . . tightened around my lungs. Like someone . . . was squeezing my throat. Like someone was trying . . . IS trying . . . to choke me."

"Have you ever had anything like this happen before?"

Falling for a Lie

"The other couple times . . . I stopped at your apartment . . . I felt like a heavy . . . darkness was closing in on me . . . and I heard voices. But it was . . . much, much worse . . . this time."

We turned a corner. "Something strange is . . . still all around me." Annette shuddered. "It's dark. It's heavy."

"I don't know why," I said, "but I think something evil is attacking you. I think we ought to pray."

We prayed for God's protection from evil spirits. The voices and oppression Annette experienced eased a little. We kept walking and praying. By the time we'd walked several blocks, Annette could breathe deeply enough that she could pray in whole sentences.

We walked and prayed, walked and talked, walked and prayed for nearly an hour. By the time we approached my apartment, Annette could inhale deeply. The tension in her face had eased. She seemed relaxed again.

Annette didn't go back into my apartment that evening. When she left, I had more questions than before she arrived. *Was the puppy seeing spirits? What is going on? Why would evil spirits want to attack Annette?*

That evening's events only added fuel to the turmoil simmering in my mind. *I don't have a problem with anything I've studied in the Bible except this last topic. Everything else I could make fit with New Age thinking. But if what I studied about death is true, what am I going to do with it?*

My insides felt as if they were boiling. *I can't go on like this,* I told myself. *I can't keep evaluating every little thing in life by both New Age and Christianity! I have to decide! Soon!*

But when? How?

I took a day off work that weekend. In my boat, I headed to a quiet cove on the lake. Anchored, I pulled out my Bible. There, I again read the texts that people used to promote immortality of the soul. I reread them, gleaning every bit of information I could to try to understand what they were really saying. Then I compared those verses with the whole body of Bible texts that related to death.

When I put all the Scriptures together, I realized that many texts stated unconsciousness after death very clearly. The few texts that some used to suggest immortality immediately after death seemed rather muddled and had to be interpreted. Never did the Bible hint that humans would have a second chance. Nothing from the first to the last page said we continued to exist right after death. But clear passages said we didn't.

Inki came out from the shade under the dashboard. She hopped up on the padded bench with me, stood with her paws on the edge of the boat, and whined. I tied a thin rope onto her collar and lowered her into the lake to cool off. She paddled about joyously. My mind rumbled with questions.

After a few minutes, Inki was back by the boat, looking up. Yip. Yip.

I hauled her in. She showered me with her shaking then settled herself in the sun.

"So," I asked aloud, "if this is truth, how would it affect what I have believed for years?"

I laid down on the bench at the back of the boat with my feet hanging over the edge. Thoughts came slowly at first. *If there is no consciousness immediately after death, there is no way we can be reincarnated into another body and pay for our sins through karma.*

Then thoughts clamored over each other as they rushed in on me. *If there is no consciousness, dead souls cannot contact us through mediums. There can be no ascended masters that can speak to us through channelers. No former Indian chiefs to pass along their beliefs in spirits and Mother Earth. No spirit forms to appear to us.*

If people live only one life before heaven, they cannot have lived previous lives. So, of course, they cannot regress into them.

"But, what about Charles Lindbergh, Jr.?" I asked aloud.

Inki thumped her tail against the boat floor.

"Ah-h-h! I can't be Charles Lindbergh, Jr.!" I basked in relief more comfortable than golden sun on a chilly day. "I'm not!"

Shortly I asked aloud, "But what about all my visions?"

A few fluffy white clouds floated slowly across the blue sky.

The devil and his demon angels saw me watching Old West movies. They could have put bits and pieces I had seen together in supposed regressions.

"And Charles Lindbergh, Jr.?"

The devil and his demon angels saw what happened with the Lindberghs and saw my interest. They could have showed me what really occurred. OR they could have made it all up. They just wanted to keep me trapped in reincarnation lies.

I reviewed the voices, the visions, the regressions. "Everything," I said aloud, "every belief in New Age depends on some form of consciousness continuing after death. . . . Satan's lie . . . that's what he told Eve . . . you won't die."

Ripples lapped against the side of the boat.

Suddenly, I paled. The bottom line hit me straight between the eyes like a bolt of lightning. "I have the same choice Adam and Eve had. Will I believe God? Or will I believe the devil?"

Chapter Twenty-nine

Last Attempt

The questions flashed in my mind. *Will I believe God? Or will I believe the devil?*

A split-second later, another thought rolled like deafening thunder. *It's more than belief. Will I serve God?* My heart pounded in my head. *Or will I serve the devil?*

Unseeing, I stared at the sky. "Oh, God," I moaned, "I thought I'd devoted my life to serving You. Never in a million lifetimes would I have served the devil intentionally." I sighed. "But I was wrong, wasn't I? I was deceived."

I had considered myself a New Age Christian. Now I realized there could be no such thing. In New Age, destiny is based on each soul's works. In Christianity, destiny is based on Christ's works. The two beliefs had conflicting foundations. I had to choose.

New Age did not build on the Bible. The Bible condemned the basic tenets of New Age. I had to choose.

New Age said my soul continued to live when my body died.

Falling for a Lie

The Bible clearly said it did not. I had to choose.

I shook my head. "God, I can hardly believe what I've done. I was deceived because I didn't use Your Word as the standard. I didn't just believe wrongly myself, I taught the devil's lies to others." I closed my eyes. Even though the sun shone warm, a chill cut to my heart. "Could You ever forgive me?"

A Bible verse flashed into my mind: *If we confess our sins, he is faithful and just to forgive us our sins, and to cleanse us from all unrighteousness.*

"Please forgive me, God," I cried. "I finally understand that Your truth in the Bible makes more sense than reincarnation. Now I see that You are a God of greater love and patience than I ever dreamed. I accept You—the God of the Bible. Please forgive me. Please accept me."

The turmoil, the frustration, the confusion of the last weeks drained away. Peace washed over me.

I can't explain what happened that afternoon. But I sensed God's love as I never had before. Not just His love for all humans through all time. But His love for me, Jay Christian—plain, ordinary person who'd made a mess out of life and hurt a lot of people along the way.

A new thought struck. Wonder filled me. "God," I said, "it's like . . . Jesus lived all my karma for me. I never have to worry about karmic debt again!"

As the days came and went, I felt an unnatural calmness. At home, I continued to study the Bible and find new and practical ways of dealing with life. At work, I handled with composure situations that would have angered me earlier.

As I continued to apply the Bible study principles Pastor Riggs had recommended, the issues became ever more clear. There are only two sources of information about God—God or Satan. The idea of reincarnation was clearly not from God. It had to be from Satan.

One evening I thought back to earlier discussions with Christians. Supporting reincarnation, I had won every argument until I ran into Annette and Pastor Riggs. *How could it be,* I wondered, *that so many Bible-believing Christians couldn't support their position against reincarnation?*

Days passed. Then one evening the force of the answer shocked me: Maybe few Christians have studied in depth what the Bible says about death. Maybe many don't know about thorough study principles, such as the ones Pastor Riggs recommended. Unfortunately, Satan uses their misunderstanding to misrepresent God's character . . . to make people think God is harsh rather than loving.

Satan also uses misunderstanding about death as a medium to present a variety of subtle lies. I remembered Pastor Riggs's comment: "Misunderstanding death makes a person vulnerable to being deceived by Satan on other issues." *I would never have given up the things I saw and heard from the spirit world if I didn't understand that death is an unconscious sleep.*

But those who don't understand. What will happen if the "spirit" of their dead grandmother, or a favorite aunt, or a respected pastor appears to them and instructs them in ways that disagree just slightly with the Bible? I shuddered, knowing how real such experiences were.

So, how important is it to know the truth about death? Understanding the truth of unconsciousness in death, I realized, *is the only protection against Satan's deceptions in New Age.*

"Oh, God," I prayed. "Thank You for leading me to truth."

Annette and Cari stopped by my apartment one evening. "We just baked some chocolate-chip cookies and we had to come to town so we brought you some." Of course I invited them in.

Falling for a Lie

Quickly! Didn't want to take any chance on their changing their minds about sharing freshly-baked chocolate chip cookies!

We visited briefly. "Well, we gotta go," Annette said. Her face was flushed.

"Are you feeling the same way you did the night we saw the dog?" I asked.

"Not nearly as bad as I felt that night," she said. "But I still feel a dark . . . heavy . . . presence. And voices are whispering in my mind."

"Have you been feeling that sort of thing anyplace other than my apartment?" I asked.

Annette looked down, thinking. Shock crossed her face. "Hm-m-m. No."

After they left, I collapsed into the orange love seat. "God," I prayed, "why would Annette be attacked when she comes to my apartment? Is there something wrong here?"

My eyes were drawn to the bookcase. A lead weight dropped onto me.

"No," I cried. "Not that!"

The turmoil I'd felt weeks before boiled up inside again. *Do I want to keep deception in my home? Will I serve God? Or will I serve the devil? The devil doesn't give two hoots about my welfare. God loves me. The devil wants to kill me. God wants to give me eternal life, eternal joy, eternal peace.*

World War III raged inside me. I wanted to run but I couldn't move.

I've allowed deception to stay in my home. Does that open the door for the devil?

I'll get the New Age books out of here. I'll give them away.

No! That just passes lies on to someone else.

I'll box them up and put them in the basement.

Why do I want to keep deception around?

"God," I finally cried, "I want You. Whatever it costs, I'll follow You."

I stood, with strength I hadn't possessed until I'd made the decision. I carried the thirty-gallon garbage can to the bookcase and pulled a backwards paperback from the shelf.

"God, you've got to help me do this," I cried.

I opened the book. Tore it top to bottom through the binding. Grabbed a section of pages and ripped them in two from side to side.

I'd based nearly my whole adult life on these books. They were my friends.

I grabbed another section of pages. *R-r-rip.* Another section.

I felt like my best friend had struggled to my door in a blizzard. And I, warm and cozy in my house, waved him away and shouted, "Go die in the blizzard. I know it's minus thirty degrees, and the wind is howling it colder. I know there's no other warm place anywhere near. You can't come in here. Go freeze to death in the storm."

Tears flowed. I slid another New Age book off the shelf. *R-r-rip.* "Help me, God."

Torn pages and book covers piled up in the garbage can. The bookcase emptied. Tears flowed. Prayers ascended.

When the job was done, I felt weaker than if I'd just run a marathon. I hauled the can to the curb. It was almost more than I could do not to grab a scrap or two for memory's sake.

In the apartment, I fell on my knees. "God, please cleanse my apartment from all the effects of the demon-inspired books I had."

In the morning darkness, the garbage truck rumbled closer, a house at a time. "God, with Your strength, I'm not going out there!" I prayed. "You love me. You won't deceive me. You only ask me to

Falling for a Lie

give up what would destroy me. You are truth, God. You are truth."

Then the crew was just outside my window. As they moved on, I heard the hydraulic cylinder and packer clunk and squeal, compressing the truck's contents.

I rolled over, tears soaking the pillow. "God, I choose You."

I struggled with my decision. *Did I do the right thing?*

The next Sunday at work I asked Annette if she'd stop by my apartment sometime in the next week or so. She and Cari dropped by several evenings later. We visited awhile. Just before they were ready to leave, Annette said, "Something's different here, Jay. This is the first time I've been in your home that I didn't feel that awful heaviness. I don't hear voices either. No problem breathing." She looked at her watch. "We've been here an hour, and I feel just fine."

A couple weeks later, I worked a long day of sales in Clarksville then met a late dinner appointment with a client. Fighting sleep on my way home, I pulled off at a wayside park to catch a nap. I leaned my seat back and fell right to sleep.

The next thing I knew, a low bass hum vibrated inside me. A dim light filled me. I couldn't move. The hum grew louder and louder. The white light grew blindingly bright. My internal organs trembled. I couldn't open my eyes. Couldn't move my arms. Couldn't speak or scream. I felt imprisoned in a body that might explode any instant.

What is going on?

My body shook from the inside. The light was brighter than any I had ever seen, and it kept getting brighter. In my mind, I could see light shining from my ears and nose, even forcing itself out my closed eyes. The hum blasted so loud I thought my body would disintegrate.

Terror filled me. Terror like I hadn't felt since the spirit had shown up in my house. I startled at the thought. *Could this be demons? Am I being attacked?*

I still could not open my mouth. Mentally, I cried out, "Satan, leave me alone!"

The deafening hum wavered.

In my mind, I screamed again, "Satan, leave me alone!"

The hum roared louder than before.

I had read there was power in the name of Jesus. Unable to speak, I trusted God to hear my prayer and work in my behalf. Mentally, I screamed at the top of my lungs, "Satan, in the name of Jesus Christ, leave me."

An electric shock jolted me. All was quiet. I opened my eyes. Darkness. I sat up and looked around. The two other cars that had been there when I arrived still were there. Crickets sang nearby. Anyone else would have thought it was a perfectly peaceful night.

"I'm awake now!" I said aloud. I started the engine and got out of there.

"God," I prayed as I drove, "I choose You. Please protect me from Satan and all his demons. Lead me to understand Your truth more fully."

Why would such a thing happen to me? I wondered. *Because I served the devil for years,* I realized. *He didn't want to let me go. He'll force his subjects into submission if he can. I'm not big enough to fight the devil. But Jesus is!*

"Praise God!" I exclaimed. "Thank You, Jesus!"

As I fellowshipped with my God on that trip home, I began to see that Satan had worked hard to keep me from learning truth. He'd tried to keep me from hiring Annette. He'd overcome me with sleep when I started to read truth. He'd attacked Annette to try to keep her from sharing and encouraging me to search for truth. He'd attacked me to try to force me back to himself.

Falling for a Lie

"Yes!" I exploded. "I made the right decision when I chose God! I made the right decision when I destroyed the books! Thank You, God, for leading me to You. Help me always to choose You!"

Life moved on day by day. It still had its stresses—work being a major one. But as I continued to search the Bible for God's wisdom, as I talked with the God of the Bible as a Friend, as I fellowshiped with other Christians who also sought truth more than convenience, I learned to trust God with my life. I began feeling an inner calm I'd never known.

I continued to sense God's love. I had never felt so accepted. So good. So comfortable meeting people. I didn't have to impress them anymore. I could just relax. Ask them questions. Find out about them.

Occasionally someone who'd known me for a while would act surprised after we'd talked a few minutes. "What's wrong?" I asked on several occasions.

"Oh, nothing. You're just . . . different."

"Different? How?"

"I don't know." Finally one person added, "I can't explain it. You're just . . . nicer."

Nicer? I didn't have a clue what they were talking about.

One evening I telephoned a friend in North Carolina who lived in the path of a hurricane. "Doug. This is Jay. How are you?"

"OK. But I'm surprised you got me. The police just let us back in for a couple hours to survey the damage and get what we could out of our house. None of us were hurt, but a tree fell through the roof and rain's pouring into the living room. It's a real mess!"

We talked a few minutes, then he asked, "Are you all right, Jay?"

"Yeah. I'm doing great. Why?"

"You don't sound like you. . . . I mean . . . well . . . don't you want to say anything else?"

"What do you mean?"

"Like, where's the sarcasm?"

Surprised, I replied, "Well, I just called to see how you were doing. Just wanted to be sure you were okay."

"Yeah," he responded, "but I've never heard you talk this long to anyone without a few sarcastic jabs. Some smart aleck remarks. It's just not like you."

Was I changing? I was enjoying life more. I didn't really see much change, but people responded differently to me than they used to.

Within weeks after I accepted the God of the Bible, I left V-105. Six months later, I returned and worked there nearly a year as a consultant. When the receptionist heard I was leaving the second time, her mouth dropped open. "You're leaving?" she asked in a tone of disbelief.

"Yeah."

"Man, Jay, I hate to see you go."

Her reaction surprised me. She hadn't said a word when I left the first time. Of all the places I'd worked, Johnson City was about the only place I'd ever gotten any heartfelt goodbyes.

We chatted a bit, there in the lobby, then she added, "You know, Jay, the first time you left . . . uh-h-h . . ." She lowered her chin and rolled her eyes off to her left. She hesitated—as if she'd gotten herself into something she really didn't want to finish.

I chuckled. "Go ahead. Out with it."

"Well . . . uh-h-h . . . frankly . . . I was glad to see you go. To be honest . . ." She hesitated, then pressed on. ". . . Well, you were a pain. But this time, I really will miss you. You have changed."

Yes, Jennifer, I have changed. I finally know the truth about God—He is love. I finally know the truth about me—I am loved.

Falling for a Lie

I can accept and serve my fellow humans even when they are vastly different than I—God loves them too. I don't have to know tomorrow—God does. I can live my todays calmly no matter how turbulent the journey—finally, the Captain of my ship is the One who stood in a tossing boat in a ferocious storm and said, "Peace."

Yes, Jennifer, I have changed. I fell for a lie. New Age beliefs nearly killed me, but the truth of the Bible set me free. . . .

Epilogue I

Life has been an exciting journey the last six years. I still love broadcasting. I continued to work in radio. Stayed in my last job for four years. Then I left (my choice) to take on a new challenge—manager of a television station.

But there's another important part of my story. Through my years in Waverly, my vow to remain single never wavered . . . until just before I left. Beyond the respect I'd felt for Annette nearly from the beginning of working together, I was growing very fond of her. After I moved away, I realized the depth of the friendship we had forged as we worked, attended church, and discussed the Bible together. I missed her a great deal. I thought and prayed about the future.

Two months after I moved, in one of our phone conversations we chatted a bit. Then I said, "I have a question for you."

"Yeah?"

"Will you marry me?"

Falling for a Lie

The phone was silent. "Marry you?" she finally asked, her voice full of surprise. "No."

She was nice about it, but disappointment hung over me like a black cloud.

Annette had been a part of my life through my whole spiritual awakening—a more important part than I'd realized. *Did I unconsciously make my decisions about the Bible to please her? Now that she's not going to be a part of my life, am I still going to follow what I've learned?*

On the heels of the question I asked aloud, "What difference does it make?"

I stood and walked to the window, looking at nothing in the darkness. "Truth is truth. God, I didn't choose You because of Annette. And I'm sticking with You. No matter what!"

Even though I felt crushed by Annette's refusal, I didn't sink into despair. I walked through the disappointment with God, secure in His friendship.

A few days later Annette telephoned. "About your question . . . Is the offer still good?"

In our Christmas wedding, Pastor Riggs made a comment that summarized my yesterdays and epitomized my hopes for tomorrow. His statement still thrills me as I watch God, day by day, fulfilling it: "God doesn't need perfect beginnings to build a perfect ending."

Epilogue II

Helen Heavirland Talks With Annette

Now, after they've been married several years, I ask Annette, "Has a new understanding of God really made any difference in Jay?"

Annette's amber eyes sparkle. She nods. Her long auburn curls bounce. "Has it ever!"

I urge her on. "How?"

She shakes her head. "He's a different person." She tips her head and looks off into the distance. "He was always polite and professional." Our eyes meet again. "You know the difference between someone who's polite and someone who's genuinely charitable?"

"Yeah."

"That's how he's changed. He was always a decent person. A good person. But he's deeper. He's real."

Annette's brows arch as she thinks. "It's hard to break the changes down into little pieces." She pushes herself back into the

215

Falling for a Lie

plush love seat. "I think the biggest change, over time, is that he became less self-centered. When you're not thinking about yourself so much, you don't get offended so easily. You don't get hurt so much. You're not as prone to be suspicious.

"He's kinder, gentler, more patient, more tolerant. Now he considers everyone else's needs. Even people who are unpleasant to him benefit from his genuine concern and desire to treat people right."

She smiles, then raises an eyebrow in wonder. "He's changed in every way—mentally, emotionally, spiritually. He's even improved physically. His joints don't hurt anymore, and he has lots more energy."

Annette seems almost overwhelmed as she speaks. "He used to be moody, easily offended, depressed. Now he's calm, even tempered. He accepts himself and others. He's positive and hopeful.

"The changes have come softly," she continues, "willingly. Kind of like a master artist is slowly resculpting him from the inside out. And he's not fighting the new design."

Annette looks at me with questioning eyes. "How has Jay changed?" she asks, thinking. She looks out the window. A moment later she answers her question. "He's a total different person." She rests her chin on her hand. Her expression darkens. "When I first met Jay, he was stressed out. He knew his business and he was good at it. But he was miserable. Now . . ." She sits up straight. Her eyes sparkle again. "Now Jay enjoys life!"

For Further Study

Essential:

The Holy Bible.
The standard for godly beliefs and practice. Weigh every idea or authority by the Bible.

Other resources Jay found valuable in his search:

Bible study guides: *Amazing Facts,* P. O. Box 909, Roseville, CA 95678-0909.
Helps for Bible study: Each pamphlet brings together a variety of scriptures on a single topic. Different topics are covered in different pamphlets.
You can study the same lessons Jay studied by mail, or on the Internet at http://www.amazingfacts.org/

Ellen G. White, *The Desire of Ages.* (Nampa, Idaho: Pacific Press® Publishing Association, 1898).
A classic on the life of Jesus Christ. Deeply spiritual and practical.

Ellen G. White, *The Great Controversy Between Christ and Satan.* (Nampa, Idaho: Pacific Press® Publishing Association, 1911).
Shows the history of the battle for your soul and clarifies Bible prophecy of future events.

Ellen G. White, *The Impending Conflict.* (Nampa, Idaho: Pacific Press® Publishing Association, 1960).
A few chapters from *The Great Controversy Between Christ and Satan.* Deals specifically with future events.

Ellen G. White, *Steps to Christ.* (Nampa, Idaho: Pacific Press® Publishing Association).
A small classic on practical Christianity.

These books, and several others by Ellen G. White can be read on the Internet at http://www.egwestate.andrews.edu/readbooks.html

Other study aids:

Will Baron, *Deceived by the New Age.* (Nampa, Idaho: Pacific Press®, 1990).
A firsthand account of the author's life as a New Age priest. It deals with his spiritual encounters and his leader's interest in the Christian church.

Edward William Fudge, *The Fire That Consumes* (Carlisle, UK: The Paternoster Press, 1994).
A detailed analysis of Scriptures which deal with hell and death.

David Marshall, *The Devil Hides Out* (Hagerstown, Md.: Autumn House, 1991).
A Christian perspective on New Age and the occult.

David Marshall, *New Age Versus the Gospel: Christianity's Greatest Challenge,* (Hagerstown, Md.: Autumn House, 1993).
Suddenly it's chic to be "spiritual." How do New Age and Christianity compare?

Roger, J. Morneau, *A Trip Into the Supernatural* (Hagerstown, Md.: Review and Herald Publishing Association, 1982, 1983).
The personal story of the author's trip into and out of demon worship.